M000315716

# ONE TWO ANOTHER

# ONE TWO ANOTHER

### LINE BY LINE: LYRICS FROM THE CHARLATANS, SOLO AND BEYOND

## TIM BURGESS

CONSTABLE

CONSTABLE

First published in Great Britain in 2019 by Constable

3 5 7 9 10 8 6 4 2

Copyright © Tim Burgess, 2019

Grateful acknowledgement is made for permission to reprint the lyrics in this book by
Big Life Management, BMG Rights Management GmbH, Kobalt Music Group, Ltd,
Mute Records and Warner Chappell Music, Inc.

The moral right of the author has been asserted.

A CIP catalogue record for this book is available from the British Library.

ISBN 978-1-47213-031-0

Book design by Nico Taylor
Typeset in Great Britain by SX Composing DTP, Rayleigh, Essex
Printed and bound in Great Britain by Clays Ltd, Elcograf S.p.A

Papers used by Constable are from well-managed forests
and other responsible sources.

Constable
An imprint of
Little, Brown Book Group
Carmelite House
50 Victoria Embankment
London EC4Y 0DZ

An Hachette UK Company
www.hachette.co.uk

www.littlebrown.co.uk

Every effort has been made to obtain the necessary permissions with reference to
copyright material. We apologise for any omissions in this respect and will be pleased
to make the appropriate acknowledgements in any future edition.

*For Morgan Burgess*

# CONTENTS

# PREFACE

So, here we are. My third book. The first was a fairly straightforward auto-biography, and the second was a vinyl odyssey, listing record shops around the world. They say stick to what you know when you write, and the words that have been a constant in my life are song lyrics. First, the words of the songs I loved, and then the lyrics of the songs we wrote as The Charlatans.

I started collecting records after leaving junior school. I found myself memorising lyrics and singing along. *Smash Hits* printed pages of song lyrics and among the words for the latest single by Howard Jones or Nik Kershaw, you could occasionally find a gem from Generation X, The Jam or Prefab Sprout. I suppose I was learning how to write songs by some sort of osmosis, absorbing phrasing, timing and other elements.

Off the top of my head, around that time I knew the words to . . .

Honey Bane – 'Girl on the Run'
Vice Squad – 'Last Rockers'
Crass – all the singles; the 12-inch EP; *Penis Envy*, *Christ*, *Yes Sir, I Will*
Zoundz – 'Can't Cheat Karma'
Dead Kennedys – *Fresh Fruit for Rotting Vegetables*
Discharge – *Decontrol* EP; *Why?* EP; *Fight Back* EP; *Realities of War* EP; *Never Again*; *Hear Nothing See Nothing Say Nothing*
UK Subs – 'Teenage'
The Exploited – *Punks Not Dead*
Sex Pistols – *Never Mind the Bollocks*, plus various singles
Cockney Rejects – 'Flares 'N Slippers', 'Police Car'
Joy Division – 'Love Will Tear Us Apart'
Section 25 – 'Girls Don't Count'
The Fall – *Bingo-Master's Break-Out* EP
Beatles – 'Yellow Submarine', 'I Am The Walrus'
Red Turns To... – 'Deep Sleep'
Buzzcocks – *Love Bites*
The Cult – 'Spiritwalker'
Orange Juice – 'Salmon Fishing in New York', 'Felicity'

Primal Scream – 'It Happens'

Dorothy – 'I Confess'

Throbbing Gristle – 'Something Came Over Me'

Wire – 'Outdoor Miner', 'I Am The Fly'

X-Ray Spex – 'Oh Bondage Up Yours!'

The Jam – 'A Bomb in Wardour Street'

The Supremes – 'Baby Love'

The Byrds – 'So You Want to be A Rock'n'Roll Star'

Pink Floyd – 'Bike'

Big Audio Dynamite – 'E=MC$^2$'

Specials – 'Too Much Too Young'

Madness – 'My Girl'

Maxine Nightingale – 'Right Back Where We Started From'

Siouxsie and the Banshees – 'Christine'

R.E.M. – 'It's the End of the World as We Know It (And I Feel Fine)'

New Order – 'Everything's Gone Green'

The Small Faces – 'Lazy Sunday Afternoon'

The Monkees – 'I'm A Believer', 'Pleasant Valley Sunday'

The Pogues – 'A Pair of Brown Eyes'

Echo & the Bunnymen 'Rescue'

Julian Cope – 'Bill Drummond Said'

Curtis Mayfield – 'Superfly'

Barbarians – 'Are You a Boy or Are You a Girl'

David Bowie – 'Rebel Rebel'

The Cure – 'The Caterpillar', 'Boys Don't Cry'

Soft Cell – 'What!'

Japan – 'I Second That Emotion'

The Beach Boys – 'California Girls'

The Carpenters – 'Calling Occupants of Interplanetary Craft'

Gary Numan – 'Cars'

Donna Summer – 'I Feel Love'

Madonna – 'Burning Up'

Fun Boy Three – 'We're Having All the Fun'
Grandmaster Flash – 'White Lines (Don't Do It)'

And lots more that don't spring to mind just now but will come to me later.

Each song had a slightly different delivery and I knew I wanted to give writing a try myself. I wasn't a naturally extroverted kind of person. I was quite shy, and still am. But seeing the singer in my favourite bands, leading their cohorts through a song or a live set, lit something up inside of me and I set about seeing if I had what it takes to be the frontman in a band.

I took my first steps in an outfit called Remagen Bridge (later to become Interzone), with Lee and Scott Turner – on lead guitar and drums respectively – and Avo on rhythm guitar, leaving bass duties and vocals to me. We played a handful of gigs, my first glimpse into the world I wanted to inhabit.

College commitments, lack of offers from *Top of the Pops* and general life/girlfriends/lack of transport conspired to put paid to Interzone. They remain mythical in the Moulton/Northwich early '80s' music scene – rumour has it that a cassette might exist with our versions of 'Ceremony' and 'A Forest'.

I retired from bass playing to fully concentrate on the duties of a frontman – with added hand gestures and microphone-stand work. My next band was The Electric Crayon Set (renamed The Electric Crayons, either by typo or by a graphic designer who thought it sounded better), another part of east Cheshire folklore.

This time my lyric skills made it to vinyl by way of 'Happy To Be Hated' (see p. 18) and 'Hip Shake Junkie'. I didn't realise it, but I was developing a style that would see me hit unseen heights with my next band – The Charlatans.

# INTRODUCTION

To update a phrase from William Shakespeare: 'Some are born lyric writers, some achieve lyric writing and some have lyric writing thrust upon them.' I am firmly in the final category. When I joined The Charlatans there was no nominated lyricist and I took on the role as a challenge.

There is no training for this job. Music is more of a science that can be studied and bettered and honed over time, but there's no standard yardstick for measuring the quality of lyrics. 'I am an antichrist, I am an anarchist' is an iconic line, but the ability to write it is natural and can't be taught. Lyric writing is something that develops over time.

There are many reasons for being in a band. It can represent an escape from your life; you might want to spend time with like-minded people; and you may harbour the distant dream of travelling the world while doing something you love. You may also find it rekindles a teenage dalliance with poetry. For the most part that youthful verse might otherwise have remained hidden away, never to see the light of day.

Before I joined The Charlatans, manager Steve Harrison asked me if I could write lyrics. I wasn't aware of any of the other members having a need to share their words with the world. I never had a burning desire myself until the role found me. I told him I would rather sing my own words than anyone else's. I was very enthusiastic, despite my lack of experience and I was willing to have a bit of a stab in the dark.

I do have a technique, if you can call it that. I write as a stream of consciousness. I find any words at all that work with the music on a first run-through and use those as a pattern to follow. I go back to look at the words again and attempt to give them structure and meaning. As I do so, I'm considering the relationship between melody, phrasing and sound – the words will at last have to fit into the mould of the music before the whole song sets.

Over the years I have disciplined myself to recognise the moment when the lyrics have set. Think of a painter finishing a picture – it's a question of instinct, to know when it's finished, otherwise the balance can be ruined.

I record the lyrics and listen back, hearing and mishearing elements that form a new version of the words. Once there is a foundation to the song, the original words fall away.

I write songs grounded in feeling rather than in anecdote.

# 'FLOWER'

*SOME FRIENDLY, 1990*

Don't bring me flowers to my bed
I don't wish you to know
It's time to find myself again
As cold as houses on your street
As hollow as my own
I hope you wish them all away

Time to say goodbye bye to the bad bad girl
Time to say goodbye bye to the bad bad girl

Don't bring me flowers to my bed
She got what she deserved

I told her I am of my time

As cold as houses on my street
As hollow as my own
I hope you wish them all away

Time to say goodbye bye to the bad bad girl
It's time to say goodbye bye to the bad bad girl

Time to say goodbye bye to the bad bad girl
It's time to say goodbye bye to the bad bad girl
It's time to say goodbye bye to the bad bad girl
Time to say goodbye bye to the bad bad girl

This was one of the first songs I wrote with The Charlatans. It grew out of a note that bassist Martin Blunt handed to me: 'Don't bring me flowers, I am not dead.' The words resonated and ideas began running around my head.

What seemed strongest was the image of me standing at the end of a bed with a bunch of flowers in my hand and the intended recipient then rejecting my kind gesture.

I was constantly thinking about established lyricists and I had an ongoing list in my head of those that I liked the most. The Rolling Stones were pretty high up on that list. I loved how the lyrics of their best songs were quite abstract – and that's what I wanted to capture, rather than songs about 'Cars and Girls', as Prefab Sprout put it. Reading the note brought 'Dead Flowers' by the Stones to mind. It has always struck me as a mean song and I guess I wanted The Charlatans to come across as a bit mean. The Sex Pistols were my heroes, but I've always imagined that if you ever got close to them they would come across as insulting. Maybe that's the biggest change in my lyric-writing since then – my meanness has mellowed and I now feel I can let my guard down.

The song revolves around the line, 'Time to say goodbye bye to the bad bad girl'. I felt I was on the cusp of something, maybe the biggest change of my life, but there were frustrations – I wanted to shed my skin but didn't know if I could. There was a gap that at times seemed too big to close. On the other side was everything I could ever dream of, but all I could see from where I was standing was the post room at ICI, the chemical giant where I'd worked since I was sixteen, and my bedroom at my mum and dad's. I didn't want sympathy or kindness: I needed to do everything myself.

I had a sense of not belonging. At twenty-one I was not quite ready for the big wide world but I was too big for the confines of the four walls of our family home. If I had been more comfortable in my own skin, I might not have had the necessary angst to write songs. People have different ways of making sense of the world and for me it was through music: punk was all about bands finding a way of articulating rebellion, boredom and a need to overthrow what was around them, while The Smiths painted a picture of isolation and encouraged listeners to take comfort in being an outsider. I loved The Fall and how Mark E. Smith used the phonic elements of words to construct a world that unfolded over thirty years for their audience.

'Flower' has recently been on my mind again. We have just lost a very good friend and it was to this song that I returned, one that comes from a lifetime ago, after it happened. I'd been planning to play solo for a while, to celebrate Independent Venue Week and to give me a chance to play the songs from *As I Was Now*. Label mates Average Sex were supporting and would become my backing band – The Anytime Minutes. We were able to keep things simple. We just needed a van, a tour manager and a friend did the merch. Touring is everything that's good about being in a band. We spend time together, play songs we love and stop off at motorway services. There are in-jokes, late-night drives and we meet some amazing people along the way.

Our London show was a sold-out gig at The 100 Club. I texted The Charlatans guitarist Mark Collins to see if he wanted to play on a couple of songs and he arrived in time for the soundcheck. It was a perfect kind of day. Many of our friends were on the guest list, including Darryl Weeks, who worked in music PR. His spirit could light up a room and he would have an effect on everyone around him. He'd flown in from Toronto for the gig and headed over for The Charlatans' North By Northwich homecoming festival. He didn't just watch, he jumped in with both feet, setting questions for the quiz that we thought would be a fantastic excuse for our fans to spend time together and get involved in something a bit different. We needed someone with an encyclopaedic knowledge of the history of the band to be quizmaster and Darryl was the most obvious choice. He came up with detailed questions that flummoxed not only the most ardent fans but even actual members of the band. He stepped in as a panel member at a conference and for ten days he was indispensable. Darryl went on to join The Charlatans on our dates in Canada and New York that year. He offered to help at my record label, O Genesis. I emailed him ideas and songs and the names of potential new artists and his enthusiasm knew no bounds.

But then came the news that Darryl had died. He had been in his hotel room for a music conference when a heart condition, that we don't think he was aware of, took him from us far too early. He was young and a husband and parent. The cruelty of this world knows no bounds sometimes. I miss him, but I cannot imagine the devastation that his family feels.

When we were writing the set list for my solo dates I had planned to do a Charlatans' song. Sam O'Donovan, the guitarist in Average Sex suggested 'Flower', one of Darryl's favourites too. I'll always think of him whenever I hear it. Once songs are out there, it's for people to construct their own stories and relationships with the words and the music. Time and again people will tell me about lyrics that I've written taking on a personal significance that gives my words new meaning.

'Flower' started off being about meanness and the desire to move on and now it's a reminder of someone who meant so much. Lyrics can be redefined over time and everyone has their own way of translating them.

# 'ALWAYS IN MIND'
1990

Have I been too long
Well how was I to know
Have I let you down
These days are silent now

This one is always on my mind
Is always, always on my mind

Why do I swim so far from the shore
Is it hard enough to catch me don't you fall

This one is always on my mind
Is always, always on my mind
I'm getting off my behind

Why do I swim so far from the shore
Is it hard enough to catch me don't you fall

This one is always on my mind
Is always, always on my mind
I'm getting off my behind

This one is always on my mind
This bag is always on my mind
This one is always on my mind

I was thinking back to songs like 'Sound of the Suburbs' by The Members and the frustrations of being tethered to my old life. 'I am getting off my behind' is me desperately wanting and willing to do anything to move on to the next stage of my life. 'Why do I swim so far from the shore' was me expressing the nerves I felt at the thought of having to leave behind pretty much everything that I knew in order to create a new identity.

# 'INDIAN ROPE'

1990

When all is wrong we have no right
Who am I to fade away

Sometimes I can tell you
What does it mean

Who am I to question why
Who am I

We come together
Follow the signs
Have you seen the size of mine

You take the blame and I'll take the fame
Who am I to sometimes say it's easy that way

You missed a good one
Give me a break
You risk your neck for something safe

You take the fame and I'll take the blame
Who am I to sometimes say it's easy that way

When all is wrong we have no right
Who am I to fade away

Sometimes I can tell you
What does it mean

Who am I to question why
Who am I

I've always loved 'Indian Rope Man' by Julie Driscoll, Brian Auger and the Trinity, and we wanted to base a song around that sound. It had a heaviness that appealed to us. The members of The Charlatans came at music from different angles and had different influences, but this was a band we all appreciated. And we had Hammond organ maestro Rob Collins in our line-up – we wanted songs that showed his strengths.

Once the music began to come together, the pressure was on to come up with some words, which I wrote during my lunch break at ICI Runcorn. 'Indian Rope' was only a working title – and if you listen to the lyrics, you'll notice that the phrase never actually crops up – but we needed to write something on the cassette. It's surprising how many of those stick, not just with us, but with other bands. I'm guessing that 'Song 2' by Blur and Nirvana's 'Radio Friendly Unit Shifter' were probably not intended to be titles on records but then they just stuck and are now perfect for those songs.

I was late to worship at the shrine of Bob Dylan. I'd been given the *Biograph* box set in the mid-'90s and, apart from his best-known songs, I'd not listened to his back catalogue in depth. But I was smitten and snapped up his albums and talked to my friends who had 'got' Bob way before I had. That's the beauty of brilliant lyric writers. Those words are there, ready in cold storage, for whenever you want to discover them. The power doesn't fade over time.

Bob Dylan most certainly had a message – I'm not as skilled with words as Dylan is and I've never been able to capture the spirit of the protest songwriter. My words have adapted to fit in with melodies and have a fluidity that allows them to be more of an extension of the music.

# 'TOTALLY ECLIPSING'

*TOTALLY ECLIPSING* EP, 2018

Remembering
All my lines to sing
Sincere in delivery
Ah-ah

Used to be
That part of me
Was in everybody else's hands
Ah-ah, ah-ah

Is this our time again
A time we really can achieve
Becoming what we could become
Or am I being naïve
We continue because we get along

Totally eclipsing from the start
Absolutely nixing on my part

When I realised it was meant to be
I fell from grace
In the same place you fell right on your face
Less speed just haste

How long has it been
Since I had a cigarette
I'm not counting
But has it been an hour yet
We continue because we get along

Totally eclipsing from the start
Absolutely nixing on my part

Is this our time again

A time we really can achieve
Becoming what we could become
Or am I being naïve
We continue because we get along

Totally eclipsing from the start
Absolutely nixing on my part
Totally eclipsing from the start
Absolutely nixing on my part

△

Often creativity inspires creativity. In May 2018, The Charlatans held our own ten-day festival, North By Northwich, in our spiritual hometown. The idea had first taken root in November 2017, while we were doing production rehearsals for a UK tour.

We hired the Northwich Memorial Court venue rather than just run through things at our studio. By the time we'd spent a morning setting up, we realised that it was inevitable that we'd be playing at least one live event there. We ended up playing four shows with other events taking place all around the town.

In August of that year we had toyed with the idea of recording an EP. Our last album, *Different Days*, had good reviews and sales; we felt that the band was firing on all cylinders. Our label agreed to put out an EP if the songs we produced were strong enough, so it was just a simple case of writing four great songs. We headed to Konk Studios, home of The Kinks, with producer David Wrench. We'd wanted to work with him for ages so our spirits were high.

Sometimes it isn't until you finish writing a song that you grasp its meaning. I always trust my instincts but that's not to say that every song makes it through to the recording studio. My wastepaper basket has always been as important a friend as my pen and the key has been knowing when to use which of them.

I sang through 'Totally Eclipsing' in my head and it struck me that although it could be about anything, it seemed to be about the band. The opening line was about getting everything together for rehearsals or a tour or a trip to the studio, while 'Used to be/That part of me/Was in everybody else's hands' referred to my old self. I had often felt like I was a commodity when I heard record company people speaking about 'shifting units' and touring 'strong territories'. It had sometimes been hard not to lose focus on what being in a band was about. I have since come to terms with the business side of things and I know that I have the most brilliant job in the world.

Part of that job is racking my brain for song-worthy material and the process can be conscious or subconscious. I have a notebook filled with words and phrases that I like the sound of. I look through it when I'm writing lyrics. There is a definite place that they come from and some find a home in a song more quickly than others.

I don't have time in a song to explain everything I am trying to convey, which is probably a good thing as otherwise they would all be twenty minutes long.

The lyrics of 'Totally Eclipsing' are upfront, positive, hopeful – a celebration of where we were as a band.

# 'HAPPY TO BE HATED'

THE ELECTRIC CRAYONS, 1989

Oh do you find me frustrating
Do you feel me nag nagging at your head
Well I am obviously underrated
Am I really so impossible to tame

Envious faces all around

Do you find me irritating
Do you feel me nag nagging at your head
Well I am obviously not backdated
Am I really the imposter in your head

Envious faces all around

I am hated

Well I am happy to be hated
Because I am happy to be backdated
I am happy to be hated ha ha ha
I am happy

Yeah

Hated faces all around

Do you feel me pulsating
Do you feel me nag nagging at your head
Well I am obviously not backdated
Am I really the imposter in your eyes

Envious faces all around

I am hated

Well I am happy to be hated
Because I am happy to be backdated
I am happy to be hated ha ha ha
I am happy

Yeah

Hated faces all around

I am hated, rated not backdated
I am happy to be hated
I am happy to be hated
I am happy sad happy sad
I am hated, hated

△

Naïve in title but all there in sentiment, 'Happy To Be Hated' is me finding my feet in a band pre-Charlatans.

Bands have been a part of my life since I was given my first chestnut Aria bass by my uncle Andrew. I was always trying to write songs or piece together ideas in a way that I could understand and more importantly that I would like or find interesting.

I have written some clangers and clankers, been unfocused and sometimes a bit shy in coming forward, lacking the conviction or confidence to give my writing the best shot, but at my best I've been involved in some absolute bangers. I've learnt to not force it and just to feel it. If it's not happening, don't worry, the muse isn't always there.

I have tried to drink the muse into focus and taken drugs to catch that elusive melody. But the best way to find a song is to wait until it comes to you. As they say, if the music is in you then it will come. See where an interesting idea takes you. Remember to enjoy the twists and turns, don't rush the outcome and don't always think big – small is just as interesting and can be more penetrating.

My songs have recurring themes: love, loss and euphoria, and many are dreamt up as smiley, throwaway oysters. But I never know what the pearl is until the audience sing along with me.

'Happy To Be Hated' was the B-side of the first and only single by an early band I was in called The Electric Crayons. It sounds confident, a bit boastful and slightly small-town, which is essentially what it is. The inspiration is writ large in the title. It was a bit of a defence mechanism against negativity. Whether The Exploited or Angelic Upstarts influenced the lyrics, the song was firmly rooted in the nihilism of many of the records in my collection.

I like to think that The Electric Crayons made it, in a parallel universe. Instead of skulking off as we did when success didn't immediately come knocking, in this alternate reality we carried on and made more records. So that means no Charlatans (or, at least, no Charlatans with me). Instead, Baz Ketley retained his job at the microphone.

The thing is, I did need to be surrounded by more like-minded people, as nice as the other Electric Crayons were. Rob Collins made me a better singer and songwriter, Martin Blunt brought experience and shouldered a lot of the responsibility, while Jon Brookes was a force of nature and Jon Baker was a nice lad and a great guitarist – but it was Mark Collins who showed us what we could become.

Everybody has to start somewhere and I was proud to start there with my songwriting, in the real universe. 'Happy To Be Hated' might not have lit up the charts, but if I could message the me working back then at ICI to say that the song would later make it into a book of lyrics I know that he would have been pleased. If I told my younger self that it was a book of my collected lyrics, he would have been overjoyed. If I'd told him that I had written the book myself, he'd have thought, What a big 'ead.

Looking at the lyrics now, they're a bit petulant and maybe a touch cringey, but they're a first attempt and a lot of what we do in our early twenties reflects who we might become later in life. But even if those lyrics might seem a little naïve to anyone looking at them now, they were part of a process for me.

# 'THE ONLY ONE I KNOW'

1990

The only one I know
Has come to take me away

The only one I know
Is mine when she stitches me

The only one I see
Has found an aching indeed

The only one I see
Has turned her tongue into me

Everyone has been burned before
Everybody knows the pain

The only one I know
Never cries, never opens her eyes

The only one I know
Wide awake and then she's away

The only one I see
Is mine when she walks down the street

The only one I see
Has carved her way into me

Everyone has been burned before
Everybody knows the pain
Everyone has been burned before
Everybody knows the pain

Everyone has been burned before
Everybody knows the pain
Everyone has been burned before
Everybody knows the pain

The classic question about songwriting is whether the lyrics or the music arrive first. In the case of 'The Only One I Know' it was definitely the music.

It existed as a fully formed instrumental and we'd already said that not all of our songs needed words. The Charlatans' back catalogue has more than its fair share of instrumentals and, even as the singer and lyricist, I was never too bothered that I was out of a job when it came to recording and playing them live. We'd been influenced by bands like the James Taylor Quartet, who didn't have a singer yet nothing seemed to be missing when you went to see them live.

We'd worked together on the music for 'The Only One I Know' and we agreed that, although it sounded great, in this case we would give words a shot. Our instrumentals have a verse-and-chorus structure that provide pointers towards the places where words could go.

The chorus was built on the style of The Supremes, the repeated notes that hit just before the chorus of 'You Keep Me Hangin' On'. It was a song that I loved anyway, but it was a cover by Colourbox that put it at the forefront. The same repetitive stabs are at the start of 'Seven Days Too Long' by Chuck Wood too. Around the same time I was also listening to 'You're Not the Only One I Know' by The Sundays a lot.

I wanted to write a big song. Something that would stand the test of time. I had thought of writing the lyrics from the point of view of someone who had been knocked down by life and love, but who refused to be defeated. It's a song about recognising that things in the present might not be ideal, but that success is the best kind of revenge. Maybe it was a song about where we were as a band – a force was taking us and guiding us and we were happy to go along with it.

The rush of writing a song means the first draft of lyrics can sometimes act as a placeholder that fits the melody. Famously, the whistling in Otis Redding's '(Sittin' On) The Dock of the Bay' was supposed to be temporary, a reminder of the unwritten lyrics for the next recording session. Tragically, there wasn't to be another session and, following Otis's death, the song was released as it was.

I'd written down the words: 'Everyone has been burned before/ Everybody knows the pain'. These two lines were supposed to act as placeholders until something more permanent was worked out. But songs set over time and words fall into place within the music. The song takes on a life of its own. I hadn't realised, but those lines were from a Byrds' song. There was a very slight change to the words and a totally different melody and delivery, but they were the opening lines of 'Everybody's Been Burned'. Like a short sample, they'd become part of our song.

I knew that The Byrds' frontman, Roger McGuinn, was aware of The Charlatans as I'd heard him speak about us while talking about a solo album on the radio. He'd mentioned young groups who had been influenced by The Byrds and had spoken about us in a very positive light. It was such a thrill to know that one of my heroes from the other side of the pond not only knew who we were but approved of us too.

'TOOIK' was always the second song that we played live – we knew there was something about it. People connected with it. At smaller shows we could see the crowd in a trance-like state – maybe ecstasy, the drug of choice around that time, had a part to play, but our connection with the audience and their connection with each other ramped up whenever we played it.

I remember driving to The Windings studio in Wrexham for the recording session, the world seemingly eager to hear what we had in store. At that point, though, it wasn't 'The Only One I Know'. Producer Chris Nagle had worked with Joy Division and New Order and the plan was to record 'Polar Bear' as our next single. My friend David 'Jonah' Jones was in the car with me. I'd grown up talking about music with him. As we approached Wrexham, fifteen minutes from the studio, I knew something was on Jonah's mind.

'Tim, I normally just sit back and watch with band stuff,' Jonah piped up, 'but I've got to say something. Not sure how it'll go down, but you should record "The Only One I Know" as the next single. There. I said it.' I nodded slowly, letting him know that I didn't think it was the worst idea and signalling for him to go on. 'It's just because of what happens when you play it. I don't know what the band feel, but I'm in there in the thick of things. It's like a religious experience.'

Jonah rolled up his shirt sleeve and held his arm parallel to his chest, showing how much the song meant to him and our audience. 'It's just like ...' He moved his arm up and down, pivoting at his elbow to mimic the swell of euphoric bodies moving in time to the bass beat. 'That hi-hat sound, then the wah-wah guitar, it's like a signal – and then, it just happens.'

His arm was moving all the while and speeding up, and he looked like he was going into some kind of trance. Jonah had connected with the song and thought if we released it at that moment, the band would reach its full potential. He made a convincing case.

When we arrived at The Windings there was a fax from our A&R man, Roger Trust: 'I've been thinking about "The Only One I Know". It has to be the next single. "Polar Bear" is a good song, but it's not "The Only One I Know". This record could seriously change things.'

I will always look on the song as representing the physical and metaphorical distance travelled to find common ground with like-minded people. The other members of The Charlatans were living in different places and we were all at different stages in our lives, yet we had to find a way of working together. It's like one of those films about a rag-tag group of army cadets who manage to become an elite unit. We have come a long way and the song has come a long way with us too.

# 'POLAR BEAR'

*SOME FRIENDLY, 1990*

World's no place to love in
She doesn't know what day it is
Freezing to death with no clothes on
Do you know what you are

It took me ages to find my way home
Give me a lead to hold on to
It's alright for you, she said faintly
You gave it away

I've never had one of those

A change of scene
Is all I need to breathe again
As soon as I thought it was over
It started again

I've never had one of those

Life's a bag of Revels
I'm looking for the orange one
She's gone
And not for the first time

I've never had one of those

World's no place to love in
She doesn't know what day it is
Have you seen my polar bear
It's that white thing over there

I've never seen one of those

How many ways, how many ways
How many ways do you fall before you're shot down
How many ways, how many ways
How many ways, do you know

I realised early on that oblique lyrics – which might seem incongruous – can end up being quite memorable. Take this line from 'Polar Bear': 'Life's a bag of Revels/I'm looking for the orange one.' There were a few furrowed brows when I first sang 'Looking for the orange one' but it ended up as the name of our fanzine and has since become a bestselling T-shirt. Case in point.

# 'SPROSTON GREEN'

*SOME FRIENDLY, 1990*

This one knows, she comes and goes
And when she goes, she goes

This one knows, she comes and goes
And when she goes, she goes

Sproston Green, she used to pace me
And now she hasn't got the time
I know I'm too necessary
And everything she stole was mine

This one knows, she comes and goes
And when she goes, she goes

This one knows, she comes and goes
And when she goes, she goes

Sproston Green, she used to pace me
And now she hasn't got the time
I know I'm too necessary
And everything she stole was mine

You've got this one, I've got no one
She's knows she's part of something wrong

Oooh

When an idea for a song arrives, at first it exists only in my head and I start to wonder, Will it ever be heard in a studio? At a festival? In a stadium? Will it be heard at all?

The most brilliant thing about writing songs with, or for, a new band is the electrical storm in my mind as I come up with ideas: rainbows, unicorns, thunder-and-lightning . . . ideas enthused over, ideas rejected.

During one of our first weekends as a band, we wrote three songs that made it on to our first album, including 'The Only One I Know' and 'Sproston Green'. Individually, we were five excitable young men looking for something to do with our lives, but together we became a creative force and we wanted to share our creativity with the world.

I can recall everything about the hour in which we wrote 'Sproston Green'. Jon, our drummer, was away on holiday but our gang still met up as we had a legendary back catalogue to create. Martin told us about a bassline he had 'modified' from a Midlands heavy rock band that he'd seen in a pub.

He played it, we loved it.

So far, so legendary.

Now for the lyrics – amazing words to go with the bassline.

At the time I was hoping for a massive change; I felt that I was on the cusp of a new life. I didn't know that it would actually happen, though, and I was nostalgic for the life I was leaving behind.

My teenage years had been filled with throwaway, responsibility-free joy. I've always loved the spirit of songs like 'Teenage Kicks' by The Undertones, celebrating the almost goofy experiences of youth, before adult life takes over: rope swings, magic mushrooms, fumbling and bumbling around, not knowing but not caring. 'Sproston Green', for me, is a time-capsule of those days, weeks, months and years, on the edge of the unknown, before responsibility and fear set in.

I was unsure how to write lyrics – I didn't know where to start. I'd seen people in clubs with notebooks, and serious kids walking by a canal, scribbling down what I was guessing were songs for their bands. I needed some help and I naturally turned to the experts.

'Penny Lane' and 'Strawberry Fields Forever' give an insight into how McCartney and Lennon drew inspiration from the places where they'd spent a lot of time. I love the atmosphere of The Kinks' 'Waterloo Sunset'. The looming fear present in 'Rusholme Ruffians' places you in Morrissey's shoes for the duration of the song. Now I am not comparing 'Sproston Green' to any of those songs, but I felt encouraged by them to tap into the motherlode that allowed memory to become song.

# 'WHITE SHIRT'

*SOME FRIENDLY, 1990*

When my white shirt lets me down
Like one we race against the wind
You said that I've seen better days
I wash her silver hair away

I'm going to be
In heaven when you say
I'm too young to waste to ever be denied
She laughed and then she died

Heard you said to me today
You're safe but you're so far away
You're beautiful how could you be so green
Tomorrow it holds the cause again

I'm going to be
In heaven when you say
I'm too young to waste to ever be denied
She laughed and then she died

And someone said to me
You've taken this too far
But I can't be arsed to change

You're so vain
You're open all day
I'm glad I got it sorted now

Heard you said to me today
You're safe but you're so far away
'Cause I'm beautiful how could you be so green
Tomorrow it holds the cause again
Again, again, again

I'm going to be
In heaven when you say
I'm too young to waste to ever be denied
She laughed and then she died

△

When I was growing up nightclubs had a scary feel. Achieving entry was a kind of holy grail. It was a rite of passage to be able to get in. Bouncers would judge you on the spot and access was only granted if you wore a shirt, trousers and the right kind of shoes (not trainers). You bowed down to their odd set of rules. As a sixteen-year-old my shirt collection was limited. In fact, it started and stopped with the white shirts I wore for school. Clubs like The Haçienda tore up the rulebooks and The Ritz on Whitworth Street hosted an alternative night on a Monday for many years. We would go and spend time with goths, punks, new romantics and pretty much any outsider group that wanted to hear music that wasn't what the white-shirted, polished shoes and cheap suits brigade were using as the soundtrack to their scuffles in clubs like Rotters and Placemate 7.

# 'THEN'

*SOME FRIENDLY, 1990*

I wanna bomb your submarines
You don't do anything for me
You were sometimes hard to find
You were never safe to be with, then

You, you're nothing next to me
I'm a phenomena you see

You were sometimes hard to find
You were never safe to be with, then

Furious again
Furious again

You don't do anything for me
We are a phenomena you see

You were sometimes hard to find
You were never safe to be with, then

Furious again
Furious again

You, you give it all to me
You never listen to a thing I said
You're furious, I'm glorious
You never hurt me that much

Many bands have been tagged with the 'one-hit wonder' label. Most of them have had songs before and after their hits, but they are overshadowed by that one huge track.

All this is tempered by the definition of a 'hit'. Our first single, 'Indian Rope', was a big, big song but it sold over a longer period of time because we were unknown when it first came out. Radio stations, clubs and word-of-mouth helped whip up sales of over fifteen thousand copies and a couple of re-presses over the months kept the sales steady, but it couldn't be considered a hit.

Now we had broken cover and all eyes were on our next single. 'Indian Rope' had only charted at UK No. 89 and without further success we would be a 'no-hit wonder'. When 'The Only One I Know' peaked at UK No. 9 we at last had the glorious, or possibly ignominious, potential to join the ranks of those one-hitters. We wanted to be remembered alongside the greats, but it was up to us to do something to ensure we wouldn't be half-forgotten alongside Althea and Donna, Renée and Renato, Brian and Michael and countless others.

It all comes down to the follow-up.

But there are different follow-ups.

In terms of what the world heard, the follow-up single was 'Then'.

But we're looking at the writing process here and 'Then' had already been written and recorded before our chart success. For better or for worse it was heading out into the world exactly as it was. 'Then' was under pressure to do well in the charts, but the real pressure for us was to write a new song.

Once finished that song would be called 'Happen to Die'. That's the one for which I felt I had to come up with something that would be written for a more expectant world.

# 'HAPPEN TO DIE'

1991

Don't give me the disease
I can't find my way out
A rush for the pleasure you deservedly honour
There's no place for the sinner in your home

Why me
Why me
There's nobody after your blood in this country
You're absolutely streets ahead of me

If you happen to die I won't be there
If you happen to believe that in order to remain there
Would you do the same on me

Why me
Why me
There's nobody's interest awaiting for no one
With all the friends I've lost I should have known

If you happen to die I won't be there
If you happen to believe that in order to remain there
Would you do the same on me

Touched by
Touched by

If you happen to die I won't be there
If you happen to believe that in order to remain there
Would you do the same on me
If you happen to die I won't be there
If you happen to believe that in order to remain there
Would you
(Do the same on me)

Once we'd had a hit record, certain elements of my lyric writing changed. I was slightly more confident. I knew people loved our music and were hungry for more. From our audience, who had begun to travel all over the world to watch us, to the record company, management and the publishers who were seeing the financial rewards, everyone seemed happy with what we were doing. But success brings more pressure – it is a double-edged sword: we were enjoying what we were doing and it was all about the songs for us, so we were spurred on to write and record as much as possible during this period.

# 'WEIRDO'

*BETWEEN 10TH AND 11TH, 1992*

Most of the time you are happy
You're a weirdo
And before the introduction ends
There is someone feeling sorry for theirselves

Look at your ugly shame
What are you talking for
Look at your ugly shame

Most of the time you're demanding
What am I doing here and I don't want to be
And the hurt in which you bare
You could say goodbye to this earth

Look at your ugly shame
What are you talking for
Look at your ugly shame
There's too much for me to know about

Most of the time you are happy
You're a weirdo
And your nerve is my device and it makes me sad

Look at your ugly shame
What are you talking for
Look at your ugly shame
There's too much for me to know about

'Weirdo' is an introspective song that seemed to chime with people and became our biggest hit in the USA. The music and the groove are really upbeat, at odds with the lyrics. Grunge had started to take over and lyrically it found a home with disenfranchised kids who had a sense that there was nothing much out there.

Rather than being about someone else, 'Weirdo' was about taking a look at myself. We'd always used 'weirdo' as a term of endearment – it was a punk thing, about being proud to be seen as an outsider.

There's a feeling I get of being enveloped in a warm sense of doom. I had it much more when I was younger, the sense of being filled with 'ugly shame' or self-doubt.

Once recorded 'Weirdo' became a call to arms, especially with Rob's keyboard riff at the start and then the runaway train of a groove. It's like the song itself can chase self-doubt out of town, for a little while at least.

# 'TREMELO SONG'

*BETWEEN 10TH AND 11TH, 1992*

The birds don't sing, they crush my skull and I'm worthless
And the heights of what I stand up to are not in you
And I can't get no words with no feeling from nothing
I don't know
Where you could ever go

(1st voice chorus)
I wonder why you bleach the sky
You could not break these strings of mine
I never knew to walk back to
A place that now belongs to you in body

(2nd voice chorus)
There I stand
My earth
Me here
In body
I stand
My earth
Me here
In body

A three-point conversation in doors with no meaning
When the world won't listen then you make your own way forward
Get out
Not going to waste outside
And I can't go where you could ever know

(1st Voice Chorus)
I wonder why you bleach the sky
And could not break these strings of mine
I never knew to walk back to
A place that now belongs to you in body

I wonder why you reach the sky
For liars and lies and turn for turn's sake
I'm never gonna walk back to a place
The place that now belongs to you – nobody

(2nd voice chorus)
There I stand
My earth
Me here
In body
I stand
My earth
Me here
In body

I stand
My earth
Me here
In body
I stand
My earth
Me here
Nobody

Our first album, *Some Friendly*, and singles felt natural to write. There were no guidelines: we were just five young men in a band, influenced by the excitement of the times, the music around us and our life experiences.

They call it the 'difficult second album' for a reason. Ours was filled with trepidation. I think this song lyrically sums up how I was feeling: crushed, awkward, exposed and battered by everything and everyone around me.

Before the first album we were answerable to nobody – we could take gigs if we thought they sounded good and we were steering our own ship. But once labels and agents became involved, we were earning money which had to feed a lot more mouths. Money had been invested in us and returns were expected. People needed to recoup. We became a bit of a product – but this is not me moaning. No, sir. We signed up for it all – with side orders – twenty-four hours a day, worldwide. But it could leave me hollow. I felt like a kid going from a kickaround in the park to playing for a big team that demanded high levels of commitment.

There was a way of fighting back: any saga we were going through could be poured into a song.

Each line of the song takes me back to how I felt and I am able to decode here what each line means. My thoughts are in italics:

'The birds don't sing, they crush my skull and I'm worthless.' *Definitely feeling a bit sorry for myself. Could well have been from overdoing it, but also I knew we couldn't any longer just record a song, love it and simply move on. Record company people, radio pluggers and people in lab coats would be prodding and poking at everything we did, hoping to maintain the success.*

'And the heights of what I stand up to are not in you.' *The limits of my patience are quite high.*

'And I can't get no words with no feeling from nothing.' *Self-explanatory for the other musicians in the band: my frustration was that if I didn't feel anything then writing songs would be beyond me.*

'I don't know/Where you could ever go.' *I was having a crisis and felt I wasn't able to help anyone else: this had always been something I'd been proud of being able to do.*

Chalk up to my confused state the idea of having two choruses. The second was sung by Rob Collins: 'Here I stand/My earth/Me here/In body.'

And the first chorus was sung by me: 'I wonder why you bleach the sky/You could not break these strings of mine/I never knew to walk back to/A place that now belongs to you.' *It was about not being a puppet to 'the man' and trying hard to stand independently. Worldwide, we were being pigeonholed and labelled and categorised – all the usual things which are just unintelligible to a young band trying to find their way in the world. Yes, we were part of something, but we were people too!*

'A three-point conversation in doors with no meaning.' *I used to invent imaginary bands with Mark and our friend John Male from Soul Family Sensation and Go-Kart Mozart. We called one of the more memorable ones Flightpath, which we thought was the most boring name for a band ever. Their difficult second album was called* In Doors. *'Three point conversation' refers to three drunken idiots – me, John and Mark – trying to make sense of poor, downtrodden Flightpath.*

'When the world won't listen then you make your own way forward.' *Yes, there was a Smiths' best-of lying around the studio and I needed a line for the song.*

'Get out/Not going to waste outside.' *My favourite lyric of the song. I will not tell the story behind it.*

'And I can't go where you could ever know.' *Obviously wanted to keep something a secret.*

The guitar break was a David Lynch/'50s-style, quite tough solo. Followed by a *Get Carter*/Harry Palmer inspired-instrumental. Followed by a Hans Zimmer *True Romance*-esque ending.

*Not sure whether true romance was out then but hey we were pioneers.*

Then going back into the chorus – the last chorus was extended and altered for the selfish purposes of wanting to keep myself interested.

# 'CAN'T GET OUT OF BED'

*UP TO OUR HIPS, 1994*

Don't let it stand out in the cold
Don't let it fall into a hole
With someone you know

Don't let it out in the cold
Don't let it fall into a hole
With someone you know

Can't get out of bed
You're keeping it straight
This city's a mess

Can't get out of bed
You're keeping it, keep on, get it together

It's everything you wanted to be
Wanted to be
Wanted to be

Don't let it stand out in the cold
Don't let it fall into a hole
With someone you know

Don't let it out in the cold
Don't let it fall into a hole
With someone you know

Won't get off the phone
You're holding the rocks
You're filling it up

Won't get off the floor
You know that we're all going off to nowhere

You're nothing that you wanted to be
Wanted to be
Wanted to be

Can't come in the road
You're filling the holes
And ruin your clothes

Can't get out of bed
It's nothing and no one's coming over to be there

It's nothing that you wanted to be
Wanted to be
I wanted to be
Wanted to be
I wanted to be

△

I wrote the words 'I can't get out of bed' on a piece of paper that remained in my pocket for a while. I'd get the paper out, read it and idly hum melody lines. I never intended to write something for cynical reasons, but I figured it's always morning somewhere in the world. I get a tweet or notification most days that a breakfast show has played 'Can't Get Out of Bed': numbers double on a weekend, as it seems to have become a lie-in anthem.

Me and Rob Collins were left at Monnow Valley Studio, Monmouth, over a weekend in the middle of recording *Up to Our Hips*. Steve Hillage was producing, but he was also on a break and we were in the capable hands of our amazing engineer and sometime producer Dave Charles. We urgently needed to release a new single and album before Rob received his jail sentence, not just because of the length of time he was going to be away but also to give him some hope. The circumstances that led to him going to prison sound even more ridiculous now than they did then and his time inside damaged him more than we knew.

We had not long got back from playing some dates in Japan and Rob, proud of the success of the band, had bought himself a BMW. He was driving near his childhood home when he saw an old schoolfriend and offered him a lift. As they approached a corner shop, Rob's passenger asked him to stop, saying he was going to rob the place with an imitation pistol. Rob laughed this off as a joke and waited outside for his old friend. The next thing Rob knew, armed police swooped on him when he got home. The former schoolmate had actually tried to rob the shop, but the owner had chased him out, taking down the licence number of the 'getaway car' – it would be funny if it were not absolutely tragic.

'Can't Get Out of Bed' was an instrumental for a long time and one that everyone liked, but we all knew that it had the potential to be a single if we paired the right lyrics with the music. Rob asked for repeated playbacks before taking some of my notes and walking into the vocal booth.

'Don't let it stand out in the cold. Don't let it fall into a hole/With someone you know' was also from the same piece of paper.

The words began to write themselves: 'Don't let it out in the cold/Don't let it fall into a hole/With someone you know/Can't get out of bed/You're keeping it straight/This city's a mess.'

The song was hastily assembled by me and Rob and I had a mental image of the sleeve of the Sex Pistols' 'Pretty Vacant' with its coach showing 'Nowhere' as the destination. That made it into the line. 'Won't get off the floor/You know that we're all going off to nowhere.'

The lyrics took about four hours to write. It's a brilliant feeling to go from nothing to something in such a short amount of time – we took the rest of the weekend off and went fishing.

# 'JESUS HAIRDO'

*UP TO OUR HIPS, 1994*

Leave us, I'm in heaven and
I can't believe I'm watching you
When everything you float upon
Comes down too soon

Jesus hairdo
I mean we all live in America
And if everything you say is true
It's bad TV

And you shine like a star
And you shine like a genius

Fix our hands together
When I surf another wave comes right
Don't want to crack, know what I need
Oh choose your words

Jesus hairdo
I mean we all live in America
And it's hard to knock reality
When you don't have a life

And you shine like a star
And you shine like a genius

Sing your song whenever
Can't you see you're catching something I need
Get yourself together now you're coming coming out of the phase

And you shine like a star
And you shine like a star
And you shine like a star
And you shine like a genius

A friend went to a book signing in 1992 and bought a copy of a novel for me. On the first page were the words:

To Tim,
Enjoy the words, thanks for the music
Douglas Coupland

The book was *Shampoo Planet* and it came as a pleasant surprise that the author seemed to be a Charlatans fan. It's always inspiring to think that someone whom you admire knows about your work. I've always been a little jealous of novelists, who can take as many words as they like to talk about a situation and don't have to try and make everything rhyme. In turn, I think they might be slightly envious that we get to shout out our work in front of an enthusiastic crowd.

I settled down to read *Shampoo Planet* and two words jumped out immediately: 'Jesus' and 'hairdo'. I wrote them down. Tyler, the protagonist, is obsessed with haircare and has a collection of different branded products. I also had a couple of notes of my own. One read, 'We all live in America' and the second was, 'It's hard to know reality'. Along with the title, I had somewhere to start.

The music had been written and recorded in Monnow Valley Studio. Rob was in prison and we were waiting for him to be released. Mark Collins's brother, John, had stepped in to play keyboards while we were writing the new songs.

From what had been recorded I knew roughly what musical lines the words had to fit. 'You shine like a star. You shine like a genius' was the foundation and it was a case of building from there.

The opening words became 'Leave us' as a change from the 'Jesus' of the very first version. The rest of the lyrics came quite easily. The song had a country blues feel and I wanted the pace of writing to match its pace.

# 'CRASHIN' IN'

*THE CHARLATANS, 1995*

All ready to get on my way
Move on up into the city today
I can see you've got a solar report
Keeps you in and keeps you boring
I can hear you snoring

One of these days you'll feel the sound of speed
And come crashin' in your flat and say
Hey, it's too late

All your friends are driving around
Coming up to feel the weekend going up in smoke
Kiss behind the coolest of walls
Standing there to kick your heart out
Oh no you've got a blow out

One of these days you'll feel the sound of speed
And come crashin' in your flat and say
Hey, come on now

I can go for miles and miles and miles and miles and miles
Oh yeah
Oh yeah

All dressed up to get on my way
Move on up into the city today
I can see you've got a solar report
You're still in and you're still boring
I can hear you snoring

One of these days you'll see the sound of speed
And come crashin' in your flat and say
Hey, it's too late

I can go for miles and miles and miles and miles and miles
                    Oh yeah
                    Oh yeah
                    Oh yeah

        See me I can feel it coming around
        See me I can feel it coming around
        See me I can feel it coming around
        See me I can feel it coming around
                    Yeah yeah

△

I was living in Salford. My first flat. We'd released three albums and we were travelling the world. All should have been fine in our lives but it wasn't: Rob was in prison – our honeymoon period was over. Reality had sneaked its way into our world.

Steve Hillage produced *Up to Our Hips* and *The Charlatans*. He was a prog legend and bands like The Orb were tapping into that world and reimagining it for a new audience. We had always wanted to work with producers who had a wealth of knowledge and experience from as many different fields of music as possible. For this song I had a vision of garage-country-psychedelic rock through a magnifying glass of arch swagger.

Steve's advice was to write as many songs as possible while Rob was away, which suited me fine as Mark and I were in the mood to get stuck into songs for the fourth album. Lyrically, this one was about keeping a flippant sneer and letting everyone know that we'd not lost what we had and that we were ready for whatever life might throw at us. We were all about positivity. We knew we were in this music thing for the long haul. We'd been accepted.

Little did we know that two years later we would face our most testing time, losing Rob and the band's whole existence brought into question.

# 'JUST LOOKIN''

*THE CHARLATANS, 1995*

I'm just lookin' to see what I'm missing
You started the riot
Ten green bottles are thrown off the hillside
You're too young to stay quiet

Find a seat on your own train
I wanna share it only with you
Gotta sail on for my sweet dreamer
They'll never take it away from you

And we stand with our hands in the air
And we're feelin' so good 'cause you care
And you're freakin' around in the bush
Feelin' good, feelin' high, it's a rush
And I'm in because I don't wanna work
In no place in the whole universe

I'm just lookin' to see what I'm missing
You started the riot
Pretty soon I'll be blowin' to match you
It's too dull and too quiet

I bet you talk about freedom
But then throw it to the sea
You better smile on for my sweet dreamer
You'll never shake it away from me

And we stand with our hands in the air
And you're feelin' so good 'cause you care
And you're freakin' around in the bush
Feelin' good, feelin' high, it's a rush
And I'm in because I don't wanna work
In no place in the whole universe

Just lookin'
Just lookin'

I bet you talk about freedom
And then throw it to the sea
Smile on for my sweet dreamer
You'll never shake it away from me

Just lookin'
Just lookin'
Just lookin'
Just lookin'

△

The lyrics were written in The Ship, a pub on Wardour Street where The Kinks and The Small Faces rehearsed. John Lennon and Keith Moon also used to drink in there, and during my time Primal Scream, The Chemical Brothers, Terry Hall, Flowered Up, Beth Orton and Liam Gallagher were also regulars.

I felt a connection between the London of the '60s and the '90s, when I sat there and wrote 'Just Lookin''. But the connection between the London of today and the world evoked in the song seems to have been lost. Independent venues and shops have been unable to survive with homogeneous glass structures of big business replacing them. No notebook and pen to write notes, everything typed on my phone.

'Just Lookin'' is a song about celebrating being in the moment. It's an anthem that urges you to be carefree and follow your dreams. It showed where the band were at but it was also a state of mind that had been with me since childhood.

The ten green bottles refer to a film I was shown in school called *Seven Green Bottles*, about misbehaving kids who meet a gruesome end after not heeding warnings of where to play and how to stay safe. We were often shown short films about the dangers of not doing as you're told – nightmare

visions of overhead cables and kites, sports days held on railway tracks –
that were way scarier than anything Hammer House of Horror had to
offer. Rather than leave me with the fear that these hideous things could
happen at any time, they gave me much more of a sense of making the
most of things.

There was always an eclectic crowd in The Ship. Like-minded people
mixed with business types and Soho voyeurs and, usually in the middle of
all this, Martin Kelly from Heavenly, his arms aloft, glass in hand, shouting
across the room – this song reminds me of him.

Who knows what someone might be scribbling down in a pub? People
who spotted me writing might have heard the finished product on the
radio a few months later and I like that thought. You never know what
someone might be writing, from a poem to a pop song or maybe even just
a shopping list.

# 'HERE COMES A SOUL SAVER'

*THE CHARLATANS, 1995*

Here comes a soul saver
On your record player
Floating about in the dust

You sing your joys baby
I'll be down when you leave
When you're free from the rust

Take your pick
Who's your saviour
Come in five different flavours

Tell me I am sweeter
Than your broken leader
I'll take the smooth with the rough

I see you lying there
Put it down
No reply in the sand in the mud

Don't kick it I want to keep it
Don't feel it I want to drive
In the sunshine of my life
In the sunshine of your life
Can you feel it when it's right

Can you feel it in your soul
Can you feel what's going on
Yeah you right

Don't kick it I want to freeze it
Don't feel it I want to drive
It's the sunshine of my life
It's the sunshine of your life
Can you feel it when it's right

Look it comes and when it flows
Like your country country song
What's going on
Going on
Going on

△

Prior to the writing sessions for our eponymous album, Mark and I decided that we needed to get away to encourage new ideas.

There was chaos in the boiling cauldron of being in The Charlatans and not much of our existence could be filed under 'regular life'. We didn't really take holidays and days didn't have any kind of format. Parties could start at 11 a.m. on a Monday and working days could be nineteen hours long. Sometimes we craved what we didn't have, and decided that a week's holiday in the sunshine was what we needed. Our girlfriends came with us and the record label booked us an apartment in a holiday resort on the Costa Brava, Spain.

Trunks were packed, suntan lotion was purchased and a plan to write at least three-quarters of an album was formulated. Following our fun in the sun, we would reconvene at my flat in Chalk Farm, polish the ideas and take them to Monnow Valley Studio where they'd become *The Charlatans*.

My holiday reading was *The Hero with a Thousand Faces* by Joseph Campbell. It became the basis for one of the first songs we came up with. Now, I'm not sure that my interpretation of the book would agree with the author's, but words and characters can clear your mind and let other ideas grow. 'Soul Saver' was about overthrowing the old for something more radical. A natural part of the order of things.

We bought ourselves a couple of lilos (as I was writing, 'lilos' auto-corrected to 'kilos': good job I changed it as that would have been quite a different outcome), we'd go to 'work' each morning, leaving the girls to enjoy the beach. Our office was sometimes a bar, often the pool and the hours were always productive. Spending time with Mark is one of life's pleasures – the thought of what song we might have at the end of a day was just about the most exciting prospect imaginable.

# 'JUST WHEN YOU'RE THINKIN' THINGS OVER'

*THE CHARLATANS, 1995*

Just when you're thinkin' things over
And you need a set of vows
And all your friends seem disappointed
To see the sun going down
And when the sweetness you're saving
Is all the sweetness you doubt

I'm coming home
You look good when your heart is on fire
It's a matter of taste yeah
You do it fine you don't follow the line
Find the sun
Ooh

I found you soaking in liquid
I found you there in your robe
Ain't no hands big enough to save us
I've got the vibe I'm coming home
I see you close up your windows
I see you burn down your throne

Yeah I'm coming home
You look good when your heart is on fire
It's a matter of taste yeah
You do it right you don't follow the line
Find the sun
Ooh

I'm coming home

Ride out, where do you come from
Kick up, go find your love
Ain't knockin' all you've done

Just when you're thinkin' things over
Oh yeah you've found your set of vows
And all your friends seem disappointed
'Cause they're not your friends now
And all the books that you've been through
Seem too sad to you now

I'm coming home
You look good when your heart is on fire
It's a matter of taste yeah
You do it fine you don't follow the line
Find the sun
Where you coming from baby

Yeah I'm coming home
I wanna build my Rome and get high
But I can't find my matches
And when you rap me you drive me to say this
Hey love, I can't sing anymore
I'm coming home...

The lines that came to me first were:

I found you soaking in liquid
I found you there in your robe

and

I want to build my Rome and get high
But I can't find my matches

The meaning might not be obvious to anyone reading those words but, then again, they weren't – and maybe still aren't – that clear to me. Sometimes lyrics are more like a mood board rather than a finished design – but those are the ones I like most.

I thought I could share my thoughts line by line:

'Just when you're thinkin' things over/And you need a set of vows.' *There's a lingering self-doubt that most of us have – it gets complex to know what code to live your life by. You know you are genuinely honest but you still might steal a towel from a hotel. We have to establish parameters for what we do. That kind of explains it, but those words would definitely not have sounded as good if I'd have actually sung them.*

'And all your friends seem disappointed/To see the sun going down.' *We were hitting our mid-to-late twenties and foolishly thinking we were quite old. People I knew seemed to be resigning themselves to the fact that their exciting years may have been behind them.*

'And when the sweetness you're saving is all the sweetness you doubt.' *Thinking that ruthless people fight harder than decent people – they have more drive and question themselves less.*

'I'm coming home/You look good when your heart is on fire.' *I feel comfortable spending time with people who are passionate about what they do, who wear their hearts on their sleeves. It's a powerful look and inspires me to do the same.*

'It's a matter of taste, yeah.' *I didn't want it to sound too preachy: beauty is in the eye of the beholder. Your opinion matters – that kind of thing.*

'You do it right you don't follow the follow the line/Find the sun.' *I wanted it to be a real anthem – the strongest mantra we had was that people should be themselves and not necessarily toe the party line. If you stick to that, you'll find your place. We'd done well by not sticking to convention.*

'I found you soaking in liquid.' *About vulnerability – someone doused in diesel, or pickled. Drenched and at their lowest ebb.*

'I found you there in your robe.' *Inspired by Gary Oldman in* True Romance *– someone so at ease with their own menace.*

'Ain't no hands big enough to save us/I've got the vibe I'm coming home.' *Once you've made your own path, you don't need to look outside for inspiration. You already have this. Home was an important idea for me as I spent so much time away. Not just the home of where we lived, but the home of our comfort zone – it was good to get back there after all the madness.*

'I see you close up the windows/I see you burn down your throne.' *A nod to reinvention. Keep changing to thrive and survive.*

'Ride out, where do you come from/Kick up, go find your love.' *Don't be afraid to look for and find what you need by searching a little. 'Kick up' was a phrase I heard a lot in Scotland. It fitted well.*

'Just when you're thinkin' things over/Oh yeah, you've found your set of vows.' *Related to that John Lennon quote that life happens while you're making other plans – everything that happens in life is all part of the bigger picture. It's to be enjoyed or at least endured.*

'And all your friends seem disappointed/'Cause they're not your friends now.' *Sometimes you have to shed your skin – people who get you and love you will come with you on the journey. They're the ones that count.*

'And all the books that you've been through/Seem too sad to you now.' *Looking back on life can make us feel wistful, but that's not all bad – we lose people. It can be hard sometimes but those are the memories that make us.*

'Where you coming from baby?' *Bob Dylan meets* The Lady and the Tramp.

'I wanna build my Rome and get high/But I can't find my matches.' *Nero was the character I had in mind. Everything was possibly to be destroyed but I knew I didn't want to do that. I wanted what we had to last forever but there was a destructive side to my personality*

'And when you rap me, you drive me to say this/Hey love, I can't sing any more/I'm coming home.' *The feeling that I'd done enough to convince whoever I was trying to convince. I'd stated my case. It was time to get on with things.*

# 'BULLET COMES'

*THE CHARLATANS, 1995*

Sometimes you cry
Cry sometimes
What you gonna do when the bullet comes round
What you gonna do when the seas are down

Lickin' like a lion
With a big cat heart
Checkin' in the dark
Bein' quick bein' smart
Live it like you love it
Do it let's go
Blowin' with the giant
Saying fe fi fo

Stuck on the way you walk
I'm hooked on the way you talk
Stuck on the way you walk
I'm hooked on the way you talk

Tell me it's the way you feel
And not the place you hold your dreams
Baby it's not where you are

Tell me it's the way you feel
And not the place you hold your dreams
Baby it's not where you are

One day we'll fly
Fly from the wack o' ma mind
Hope you're here to stay to see the bullets come round
People working out with their sun hats on

Kiss me like a tiger
With a big cat heart
I'll read it if you buy it
Bein' quick bein' smart

Lookin' at the devil
Fuck it let's go
Blowin' with the giant
Saying fe fi fo

Stuck on the way you walk
I'm hooked on the way you talk
Stuck on the way you walk
I'm hooked on the way you talk

Tell me it's the way you feel
Not the place you hold your dreams
Baby it's not where you are

Tell me it's the way you feel
Not the place you hold your dreams
Baby it's not where you are

Live it like you love it
Live it like you love it

Live it like you love it . . .

△

Mostly either the music or the lyrics come first, but on rare occasions they arrive simultaneously.

The band share writing duties and sometimes Martin or Tony come in with music, or Mark and I might meet to come up with some songs – although not always on holiday in Spain. At times I have writer's block and inspiration doesn't come. Sometimes a song can hit me near fully formed at any time, even while cleaning my teeth.

It was drummer Jon Brookes who provided the inspiration for 'Bullet Comes'. He instructed the rest of us to listen to *Gris Gris* by Dr John, the

'Night Tripper'. The idea was to summon a New Orleans voodoo gumbo, and he must have also spoken to our photographer of choice, Tom Sheehan, as he appeared with a staff adorned with percussion bells and mini-cymbals for Jon to play. If anything was going to conjure spirits, it was this spooky stick.

The beat mixed homemade loops and Jon's precise, off-kilter fills. I was listening to *Fly* by Yoko Ono and included quite a lot of Sly Stone influences. Listening to it now, I also hear echoes of Beastie Boys and Mick Ronson too. It's a concoction of gargantuan proportions.

Some songs demand more of me in writing lyrics, and I know I felt the pressure with this one. I felt drawn to words that conveyed the idea of living life to the full, being able to find love and hoping to keep hold of it, and not being frightened of embracing life. 'Live it like you love it' was Jon's idea, and it's a mantra to be repeated until it finds a way into your heart.

When I am writing lyrics I like to document everything around me. The tiger in 'Kiss me like a tiger' was a reference to a hot water bottle cover rather than a ferocious animal; the picture of the bottle was adapted and used for T-shirts and badges.

I wanted the lyrics to be like a boxer's jab. One after the other – hopefully all on target – with the next along any second, bobbing and weaving until we found the groove of the song.

# 'TELL EVERYONE'

*THE CHARLATANS, 1995*

(Just run through it)

Tell everyone
Don't put it on
It makes no difference to me

Won't mess around
Been there so long
It makes no difference when you smile

'Cause I don't run from love from anyone
And I can land on money or the moon

On hillside straights
Can't walk it's late
I know that something's left alive

Well, I don't take no shit from anyone
And I can land on money or the moon
You know the sun will come soon
And we can sail away
Away

Tell everyone
Don't put it on
It makes no difference to me

'Cause I don't run from love from anyone
And I can land on money or the moon
You know the sun will come soon
And you can see you're there for me

Song lyrics sometimes change slightly in a recording: to make them scan, because they sound clunky, or for any other reason. Occasionally elements of the studio's background buzz – background chat or laughter – are kept, which I've always liked as they create the illusion that the listener might be sitting in on a recording session rather than only hearing the final product. Bob Dylan, New Order and Gram Parsons are among those who use this approach.

The first words of 'Tell Everyone' are 'Just run through it' and then we get into the song. This is a song about being yourself, being loyal and being happy – it conjures up memories of walking home at night in the rain, smiling, without a care in the world.

Edward Lear-inspired rhyming comes at a point in the song where everything is beautiful without needing to say too much.

The choice of 'money or the moon' comes from dreams of being a spaceman as a kid or idle moments spent wondering what life might be like if you won the pools or the lottery. Yet the song also deals with what you might do if another hand was dealt. It is ultimately about positivity in the face of whatever might come along. People often say that, of all our songs, it's the one that makes them smile.

# 'LIFE IS SWEET'

*EXIT PLANET DUST, 1995*

Days like this are sweet
I'm talking in my sleep
I think you're going soft
I know what's there for me

On Saturdays I shop
I'm walking with my dog
Life's a canyon size
Break up the sun there's nothing bad in my life
Loaded out on love
Break up home there's nothing up with me

Driving in the sun it's a hell of a way down south
Bring me back my love I'm tidy in your home

On Saturdays I shop
I'm walking with my dog
Life's a canyon size
Break up the sun there's nothing up with my life

Loaded out on love
Wake up home there's nothing up with me

Days like this are sweet
I'm walking in my sleep
This place where I belong
I bang a million drums
Someday I'll go back home
You'll get up and go
I like it in my head

I am caught up in your love . . .

I've always loved the parallel lives of The Charlatans and The Chemical Brothers. We had our own worlds and occasionally they would meet. Mostly they came over to our side of the fence, temporarily leaving their club habitat to remix our guitar-driven hits but, in making their first album, Tom and Ed sent over two pieces of music, asking if I fancied adding lyrics and singing on whichever of the two I liked more.

One jumped out as a song I thought I could sing on – I felt the other was already quite complete: it made it to the album as an instrumental. The music was a hundred per cent finished and that meant I knew exactly what I had to work with. I'd recently watched Mike Leigh's *Life is Sweet*, and that struck me as a great title. I've always loved Pet Shop Boys lyrics. Sometimes they refer to really everyday occurrences to accompany the most amazing dance music: a song like 'Left to My Own Devices' mentions waking up and drinking tea.

I had the music, care of the Chems, and the words came easy: 'On Saturdays I shop/I'm walking with my dog.' It was like having a holiday romance with The Chemical Brothers, something I didn't think would come round again. But four albums later a new instrumental hit my inbox – we were about to get the band back together. There was no title attached to the new music but they did give me a few notes about a hustler and 'can't shake this feeling': the idea seemed to be well on its way. It just needed a few laps around the block and a few rounds in the ring. It found itself the title of 'The Boxer' and the completed song was included on their 2005 album, *Push the Button*.

# 'ONE TO ANOTHER'

*TELLIN' STORIES, 1997*

One to another, sister and a brother
And they're changing the way that you feel
Pleased to meet you, hope I never see you
I'll be at ease watching you sleep, watching you smile

Love, I adore you
Always looking for you
And I'll be there whenever you need me
Be my Spiderwoman, I'll be your Spiderman

I hear our day is coming
It gets sweeter every year
Tomorrow could be too easy
And today's going to be too near
Trust is for believers and love can keep the faith
I don't need you, I can't buy you, I can hurt you

One to another, peace to my brother
Always giving me his thing for free
Sad to knock you, it's good to rock you
And I'll do it the best that I can

I hear our day is coming
Gets sweeter every year
Tomorrow could be too easy
And today's going to be too near
Trust is for believers and love can keep the faith
I don't need you, I can't buy you, I can hurt you

Stand by my accusations
I'll come clean, I don't need no vice
I know you want to keep me waiting
I think it's funny that you might
Love is hard to leave and it's hard to never have

Can you please crawl out your window
You can play with all my love, yeah, yeah, yeah
Box up all my records and a head full of ideas
And a hand full of escape routes, they're going to burn you

△

I am guessing the line that I'll be best remembered for is, 'Be my Spiderwoman, I'll be your Spiderman.' Now I know it's no 'The answer, my friend, is blowin' in the wind' by Bob Dylan, but I don't make the rules. More than once, I've been shown tattoos and clips of wedding vows that feature those lines, that came to me while I was on a train from Paddington to Newport to meet Mark, Rob, Jon and Martin at Rockfield Studios to work on the song.

Bad ideas can start off as good ideas and I wasn't sure which kind 'Spiderwoman'/'Spiderman' would end up as. Judging by the enthusiasm with which it gets sung at gigs, I'm saying it arrived as and remained a good idea.

I'd recorded a guide vocal which, in my case, could often be a jumble of random words or the word 'blah' repeated or even sections of humming. I had most of the lyrics sorted, but I wanted the song to be about the theme of connection, and to use words that could be sung in an anthemic style.

Coming up with the first line of a song – not necessarily the opening line but the one that kicks everything off – is a big moment. But as with a jigsaw, it's putting the final pieces into place that gives me the greatest satisfaction. I remember the band's reaction to the 'spider' lines included the odd raised eyebrow and furrowed brow at first, giving way to purposeful nodding and a chorus of, 'Yeah, I like it.'

I like the swagger of 'Pleased to meet you, hope I never see you'. It's not meant to be cocky. I had a connection with my bandmates and our fans – they were the ones I was there for – but it was how I felt about lots of the people in the business side of the music world. I don't want to sound mean or dismissive but it was good to express the way I felt.

At the time, we were prolific: 'North Country Boy' and 'How High' were written on the same day and within a week 'One to Another' arrived.

I didn't overthink the lyrics too much – those songs also variously featured Itchy and Scratchy from *The Simpsons* ('North Country Boy') and Caine from *Kung Fu* ('How High'). Looking back, I think I must have been watching a lot of television.

# 'NORTH COUNTRY BOY'

*TELLIN' STORIES, 1997*

Hey country boy

Hey country boy
What are you sad about
Every day you make the sun come out
Even in the pouring rain
I'll come to see you
And I'll save you, I'll save you

What do you care about
And she says 'this and that'
What do I mean to you
I'll show you if you want the truth
I can't remember
I don't know how to tell you
But I love you just the same

How many eyes must a young girl have
I know she makes you cry
I know she makes you laugh
I'll be good to you if I could I'd make you happy
If I had a son I'd be good to my daddy
Who loves you though I bet it's not the same
As your North Country Boy

Hey country boy
What are you sad about
I think we'll work it out
Even in the morning rain
He'll come to see you
Hope your feelings are the same

How many ears must a young girl have
I know she hears you cry
I know she hears you laugh
Itchy and Scratchy come runnin' up the alley

If you'll be good I'll be good to your daddy
Who loves you but I bet it's not the same
As your North Country Boy

What do you care about
And she says 'this and that'
What do I mean to you
I'll show you if you want the truth
I threw it all away
I don't know where I put it
But I miss it all the same

How many eyes must a young girl have
I know she makes you cry
I know she makes you laugh
I'll be good to you if I could I'd make you happy
If I had a son I'd be good to my daddy
Who loves you but I bet it's not the same
As your North Country Boy

△

Some songs make a specific connection that puts them into a new context after they are written and recorded. It can happen with a memorable performance or, as with 'North Country Boy', the filming of the video.

The song was written at home in Chalk Farm, finished in Rockfield Studios in Wales and confirmed as the follow-up to 'One to Another'. It was to be the first record to be released after the devastating loss of Rob Collins in an accident. Following his release from prison, Rob had returned to the band and was in the middle of working on *Tellin' Stories* when he was killed while driving his car near the studio. When it came to releasing singles a few months later the rest of us were still in shock but we had to carry on. That meant shooting a promo.

Our budget in those days was in the region of forty thousand pounds. Only a tiny number of acts would get even a quarter of that today – if you allow for twenty years of inflation, it shows how mad things were back then. We didn't have an idea for a story or a theme: we were not in the headspace. We just wanted to spend time together; to get away from it all. Fortunately, the director was a long-time friend, Lindy Heymann. We knew we were in safe hands and she would want to do what was best for the band – then we had the idea.

The budget would cover the cost of flying all of us, plus a camera operator, to New York, get us an amazing hotel to stay in (The Soho Grand) for nearly a week, and pay for food, drink and sundries too. The only issue was that there was no money for locations or people in front of – or anyone else behind – the camera. We had literally seventy-two dollars left which we joked we'd use to pay for a cab. And that's what we did. We walked around New York and filmed ourselves taking that cab ride.

The starting point for the song itself was the title of Bob Dylan's 'Girl from the North Country'. People are intrigued and ask me about the mystery of the identity of the protagonist: after my relationship with a girl from the north country broke down, I just wanted to let myself know that I was still here. Much of the lyrics concern messages to myself. I was trying to put my life in order, hoping that my own experience would ring true with listeners.

Listening back now, the line that resonates most is, 'If I had a son I'd be good to my daddy'. I do have a son now, and he has made me rethink so many things about my relationship with my own father. This has been a positive process that gives me the perspective to see clearly what I mean to him and what he means to me. Having said that, it's Itchy and Scratchy from *The Simpsons* that I get asked about most when talking about this song. As with 'Spiderwoman' and 'Spiderman' in 'One to Another', there seems to be a pattern here: my most remembered lyrics often reference cartoon characters.

# 'TELLIN' STORIES'

*TELLIN' STORIES, 1997*

Come see me in the mornin'
Can't you see I'm tellin' stories
My sweet angel's everlasting true love ways

I'll wait I'll sow the seed
I'll set the scene and
I'll watch the world go by

See me go through changes
Revelations to blank pages
I'll find a brighter guide to see me through
And leaves fall to the ground
Turn to brown through the day just like you

Live for the day
I see your heart is empty I've got plenty
Joe come ride with me
I see your head is meant to be cemented
It's true
When the stories that you tell come back to haunt you

I'll be there in the morning
Can't you see I'm tellin' stories
My sweet angel's everlasting true love ways
While others turn to others
Introduce you and walk right on through

It's just about knowing where you come from
Being you and singing love songs
Can begin to fill your day

I could lead you to the top don't stop
I could lead you there still

Live for the day
I see your heart is empty I've got plenty
Joe come ride with me
I see your head is meant to be cemented
It's true
When the stories that you tell come back to haunt you

△

I had a special connection with four people while writing this song. All four were named Joe (one spelt 'Jo'): Martin's dad, Martin's son, a childhood hero and the partner of a band member – who was mum to his daughter and sadly soon to be his widow.

'Tellin' Stories' was the fourth single and the title track of our fifth album. Our live shows had taken a step up from bigger theatres to arenas and, in some ways, we were at the height of our powers. But in others we were the weakest we'd ever been. We'd lost Rob towards the end of recording, and yet the album went stratospheric on its release. The writing of the lyrics of 'Tellin' Stories' dates back eighteen months before the tumult.

The band were in fine fettle, our eponymous album had gone to UK No. 1 and there was no shortage of new material. Mark and I decided to head to Windermere in the Lake District to start writing what would be our most successful album.

Mark's set-up comprised:

1 x acoustic guitar
1 x electric guitar
1 x bass guitar
1 x Portastudio

My toolkit consisted of:

1 x pen and pile of paper and a stack of CDs for inspiration.

If our tools of choice were the engine, then the fuel was Stella Artois,

Marlboro Lights, port, brandy, weed (skunk) and Laurel and Hardy ('Tellin' Stories' was originally 'Laughing Gravy', after the dog in the eponymous short film). I had a bout of food poisoning from a curry that made me a bit delirious, but I made the most of the delirium – sometimes it can be a gift. Kenn Richards, our long-time friend from NYC showed up to check out the sounds and give his much-valued opinion.

We wrote 'Don't Need a Gun', although it was quite different and titled 'Rainbow Chasing', and 'With No Shoes', as well as 'Tellin' Stories'. Mark said the lyrics of what was then 'Laughing Gravy' made me sound like a teacher. This was a completely new reaction and I had to check whether he meant that in a good or bad way – after all, I've always been a fan of new situations. He was referring to 'See me go through changes/Revelations to blank pages/I'll find a brighter guide to see me through.' It was as close as It was closely inspired by *John Wesley Harding*-style Dylan, which had been hogging my turntable. It ended up sounding like The Charlatans, but the best possible version of The Charlatans.

# 'DON'T NEED A GUN'

*TELLIN' STORIES* REISSUE, 2012

I am on an epic trip through time
Don't need a gun to blow my mind
These images of diehard's fasting

I want to be the first
Can't be no second third or fourth
And I don't give up on chasing rainbows

Live long my darling be my friend
I know I'll be here till the end

I am going back to your hometown
Where microwaves turn young mothers on
And new ideas float down the river

You gotta say what's on your mind
I know the truth is so unkind
You're the seventeenth mostest cruellest winter

Wake up my darling be my friend
I know I'll be here till the end

Our love is enough to keep us
I took you to the stars

Live long my darling be my friend
I know I'll be here till the end

Whenever I talk to anyone who saw Rob play, they always comment that they had never seen anyone quite like him on the keyboards. I am not saying that they all said he was absolutely the best technically – but he was uniquely brilliant.

After his death we knew we had to finish *Tellin' Stories*, whether we continued as a band or not and, for a while, the work kept us occupied and, almost, distracted. After we finished the album, though, the future loomed over us with a question mark.

What next?

It was Felt and Primal Scream keyboard player Martin Duffy who drove us on, sitting in while we searched for a new member. Mark and I remembered a song from our Windermere writing sessions called 'Rainbow Chasing' – the song that turned into 'Don't Need a Gun'. It was an upbeat number that had been written before Rob's death and we wanted it to have a more sombre feel. It was important that we were respectful and we wanted the next music we released to reflect that. We didn't think that a skip-along tune was right.

We shared the original version with the *Tellin' Stories* reissue, a reference point that demonstrated the way a song can change. Ironically, the song was about keeping going in the face of adversity: maybe it had been a message to our future selves.

Lyrics can be time capsules that you have to revisit many years later in order to uncover what they were really about. Writing is a form of therapy, but you may have to pick through your words to understand what you were trying to say.

# 'HOW HIGH'

*TELLIN' STORIES, 1997*

How high
Oh! I can kiss the sun
Run a minute mile
While you hitch hike
Love shines a light
I'm a loving cup
And I'm looking for the one who cut you up
You're not having me
You know the skies are mean
I'm looking for a way to free you love

I'm fixing holes
The ones you break up
Come in from your drive
And the hand that rocks you
Cuts you up like
Lyrics of your life

I can't buy
What I've done before
I want to open up another door
I'm going to let you pass
On another path
I want to be the king
While you zig zag
On a holy road
Like Caine from *Kung Fu*
How high
Oh! I can kiss the sun

Hang on to your hopes my darlin'
Don't let it slip away
And the hand that holds you
Keeps you warm
And helps you live today

Love shines a light
And it takes and it hurts
I know I'm right
I can bend till I burst
And love shines a light
And repays you with us
Yeah too right
I'm gonna pledge my time till the day I die

How high
Oh! I can kiss the sun
Run a minute mile
While you hitch hike
Love shines a light
I'm a loving cup
I'll be down when you're down
I'll be up when you're up
You're not having me
I know the skies are mean
And I'm looking for a way to free you love

I'm fixing holes
The ones you break up
Come in from your drive
And the hand that rocks you
Cuts you up like
Lyrics of your life

Love shines a light
And it takes and it hurts
I know I'm right
I can bend till I burst
And love shines a light
And repays you with us
Yeah too right
I'm gonna pledge my time till the day I die

It's so hard to pin down what makes a great song, which makes it incredibly difficult to try to set out to write a great song. Of course, there are people out there who may say that I've never written even one great song but, for the purposes of this book, let's assume that I have at least managed to produce a couple.

Songwriters are constantly on the lookout for inspiration, but that doesn't mean that, after twenty minutes of work, the tenth sheet of paper isn't hitting the bin. Inspiration can come from any direction. Chic getting turned away from Studio 54 gave us 'Le Freak', Dolly Parton's decision to leave her songwriting partner with a parting gift meant the world gained 'I Will Always Love You'. The jumping-off point for a song can come from different emotions and the lyrics can be driven by a certain mood. 'How High' came mainly from a place of frustration but that was as good as any place to start.

A band of young upstarts by the name of Oasis had arrived, made themselves at home and become the biggest band in the world in the space of two years. They had planned a couple of hometown shows in April at Maine Road, the home of their beloved Manchester City. Word came through from the promoter that we were being offered the support slot – we'd be playing in front of an audience of forty thousand. But we had an album to write and me and Mark are United fans. It was a tough decision to knock it back and although our heads said 'Maybe', our hearts said 'No'. We would go on to support Oasis at neutral venues such as Knebworth and Finsbury Park but it had to be a 'no' to Maine Road – so, yes, we had some frustration at turning down a big gig. But we also had a place to channel that frustration.

I was playing a lot of De La Soul's cut-and-paste classic *3 Feet High and Rising*, as well as Bob Dylan, at the time. No one really picks up on it, but *Tellin' Stories* contains our homage to rap. 'How High' is my head processing these different styles and I think the result went down well. There was a hidden gem on *3 Feet High* called 'Tread Water'. Its lyrical style lay somewhere between stream-of-consciousness and nursery rhyme and that really appealed to me. I wanted to write a song with the punch of the Wu-Tang Clan but with the playfulness of De La Soul. While I liked Wu-Tang Clan there was no way I was going to start rapping about my suburban life and the delicatessens of Didsbury, where I was living at the time, but I wanted a song that captured the pace and the ferocity of their music with some hood lyrics.

Method Man and Redman had a song called 'How High' in which the words and references breathlessly piled up. It seemed to be driven by a sense of frustration that I could feel in the performance of the song. It was hard to keep up with them. I wanted a song that was like that, that was like a runaway train. I wanted to start the song with those two words, but at that point had no intention of using them as the title. Now the song was getting started . . .

I might not have been about to take up rapping but I'd always been struck by the way Dylan sang songs like 'Subterranean Homesick Blues', the beat of the words deciding the direction of the song. Almost cut-up style. I wanted a chance to channel the arrogance of a rap song and sing as a character rather than the shy person that I am. 'How High' is about everything ever, condensed into three minutes and eight seconds.

Wu Tang's obsession with Shaolin references crept in. I was no expert, but I channelled Caine from *Kung Fu*, the '70s' TV series with David Carradine. I wanted a relentless barrage of words, but I knew I had to get my breath back. I love 'Barstool Blues' by Neil Young with its beautiful section at the start, when he really aims for high notes that show the fragility of his voice. I had it in mind for the lines, 'And the hand that rocks you/Cuts you up Like/Lyrics of your life.' This was a nod to the cut-up lyric style I was using. I was a big fan of William Burroughs who sliced not only sections of text, but audio tape too. I'd read about David Bowie doing it when I was a kid and it was something I'd always wanted to try.

The next step was to share what I'd written with the rest of The Charlatans, at Rockfield and Monnow Valley Studio, where the rest of *Tellin' Stories* was coming together. Mark wrote the guitar parts on his Gibson Les Paul and played it through a Vox AC30. Jon matched the urgency of the words with an unapologetic drum beat and the song formed pretty quickly.

I had always kept notebooks, even before The Charlatans, and I would refer to them to keep the ideas moving along. While we were touring we would have a stack of videos to watch on the bus, I would scribble down phrases and ideas as I watched. 'Fixing a Hole' is a Beatles song from *Sgt. Pepper's*, and the title must have been on my mind at the time.

There is a scene in Michel Gondry's *The Science of Sleep* in which a character explains how dreams are prepared: first, take some random thoughts, then add reminiscences of the day and mix them with memories from the past – love, friendships and relationships. Songwriting is a similar process for me. I pull together the things I see and hear during the day and combine it with my personal stuff. When I watched that scene it felt like a glimpse of the inside of my head in songwriting mode. Not everyone writes in the same way, obviously, but I certainly mix everything up, a recipe crossed with a science experiment.

The final part of the 'How High' story features our journalist friend Emma Forrest. She went to Germany to interview Wu-Tang Clan and asked Method Man if he'd like to hear a song they had influenced and for which they'd unknowingly provided the title.

'Sure,' said Method Man. Emma played a cassette with 'How High'. He leant back, took a huge drag of his philly blunt and said, 'It's cool.'

Job done.

# 'HOW CAN YOU LEAVE US'

*TELLIN' STORIES, 1997*

Darling, don't you cry, whatever is yours is mine
All the pictures on your wall, I know you look up to them all
Usually love comes first, I watch as you twist and turn
I could give you mouth to mouth and only the truth would come out

Here I come, how can you follow
It's only a gut feeling
I don't want to believe it
How can you leave us
How can you bleed on us

Darling, you live to learn, hanging on all our words
Promise me you'll be home soon, I could rush through the city to you
Won't find you in this world, catching dinosaurs
No saint will save you this time round
I only wish you were here with us now

Here I come, how can you follow
It's only a gut feeling
I don't want to believe it
How can you leave us
How can you bleed on us

How can you leave us
How can you bleed on us
How can you leave us
How can you bleed on us

Some songs make an indelible, specific link. It could be you remember where you were when you first heard a track or perhaps something memorable happened. In my case, writing 'How Can You Leave Us', it's the title that brings back a moment. I didn't think of it while wandering lonely as a cloud – the phrase was shouted loudly in my ear by a friend as Blur left the stage after their Montreal gig.

The Charlatans were touring with Menswear in support in Canada in September 1995 and we had a night off at the same time as Blur were playing. It might seem like taking a bit of a busman's holiday but I've always enjoyed going to other people's gigs while on tour. I went with Robin Turner from Heavenly and a *NME* journalist and we bagged ourselves a few spots on the guest list.

Blur's set was a typhoon. The stand-out songs for me were 'The Universal', 'End of a Century' and 'Girls and Boys'. Their star was rising and didn't look like it was going to stop. I enjoyed myself, but I'm not sure how I would describe Robin's experience: it was something akin to possession, complete with rolling eyes and speaking in tongues. As the band said their final goodbyes, Mr Turner returned to his earthly state, shouting repeatedly, 'How can you leave us? How can you leave us?'

It struck me as the perfect title for a song, though it gained unwelcome poignancy when Rob died within a year of us having begun work on the track. So many people think it's about Rob's death, but he wrote the piano parts and did play on the recording.

# 'TITLE FIGHT'

'HOW HIGH' B-SIDE, 1997

Whatever helps you through the night
My paws keep going to turn on the satellite
Always look for the positive
I don't feel the pain when I'm watching the title fight

How could I ever want to disown you
I want to love and to have and to hold you
All the good in the world and you keep it under your thumb

Amphetamines will keep you thin
My heart beats fast and I'm climbing the walls again
I've been talking for miles on end
Or is it because everybody is a friend

How could I ever want to disown you
I want to love and to have and to hold you
All the good in the world and you keep it under your thumb

I have my freedom and while I'm living
I know the world can't touch me
I could wait forever, love in vain, yeah
I'll have you when your birthday comes

I am the Sundance Kid coming to you
In the groove and I'm positive
Is it because our talent's shining
Bound by the empire, follow the Eskimo

How could I ever want to disown you
I want to love and to have and to hold you
All the good in the world and you keep it under your thumb

I have my freedom and while I'm living
I know the world can't touch me
I could wait forever, love in vain, yeah
I'll have you when your birthday comes
What a way to go

I have my freedom and while I'm living
I know the world can't touch me
I could wait forever, love in vain, yeah
I'll have you when your birthday comes

△

The only Charlatans song to feature three keyboard players: Rob Collins, Martin Duffy and Tony Rogers. People often ask why it didn't make it on to *Tellin' Stories* and the simple answer is that it wasn't finished in time.

I always thought that 'Title Fight' was a great name for a song – and, trust me, they're harder to come by than it might seem. All of the good ones are usually taken, clichéd, or are so good (like 'Help', 'Heroes', 'Blue Suede Shoes') that the tune has a lot to live up to.

'Title Fight' is what I call a stoner song: you have to inhabit the brain of the person in the song to appreciate it fully. I usually write this kind of song in a cut-and-paste style – not necessarily snipping from a magazine, but scribbling down random words as they are generated in my head. I have to be loyal to them, even if they don't make sense the first time I read them through.

The pre-chorus is like a vow and it still reminds me of the emotional headspace I was in at the time. I felt scattered and my job left me exposed. Songwriting was the thing I loved to do most in the world, but I was broadcasting my innermost feelings and questioned why anyone would want to know me so intimately. I have always felt the turmoil of writing, the whole process of digging down deep emotionally and then delivering my feelings with a swagger that doesn't come naturally.

For the most part, I'm quite shy. Most of the bravado of early interviews was either Dutch or often Colombian courage – I built up worrying dependencies on both as I found they provided a way around my natural state of not really wanting to be the centre of attention. Over the years I've managed to figure myself out and I've kind of reconnected with that quieter side of me and it's a process I've enjoyed. I realised I never really needed the drink or the drugs. It took a while for me to get there though. I was looking for stability that became ever harder to find the more successful we became.

I'd always loved the romantic idea of partners in crime in films from *Bonnie and Clyde* to *Thelma and Louise*. The Sundance Kid makes an appearance here, but without Butch Cassidy. I wanted the song to be an upbeat declaration and hopefully it is that.

'Bound by the empire, follow the Eskimo.' The empire isn't a *Star Wars* reference, but a reference to the way record labels worked and how we were bound by their methods, despite our natural instinct to be self-contained. As a kid I loved the idea of being an Eskimo – 'Eskimo' now might need to be replaced by 'Inuit' – because I was impressed by the way that as a people they travelled light, built temporary homes out of what they could find and survived by working together in a hostile environment.

# 'FOREVER'

*US AND US ONLY, 1999*

Forever you're my foundation
I know I can keep
Told I was good for nothing
Branded a cheat
Now I know why you listen
I can help you anytime
Love is all there is
I don't know what you people do with your lives

Hey, oh I wonder what you people do with your lives
Oh, I wonder what you people do with your lives
Oh, I wonder what you people do with your lives
Once more this will be forever

I can't withhold secrets
I know I'm going where the sun always shines
I know my son, we've made it
It can't escape my mind
I know my star, I know my star
Is a brighter star, brighter star
Forever be in my arms
Forever be in my arms

This could be a myth in the making
Under a spell
Down to ambition
I guess you could even call it a miracle
I see my true love coming
My little bundle of joy
I can help you realise
It's us and us only

I know I'm as good as my neighbour
A starter for ten
I can't promise I'll always be with you
I promise I'll always be there

Oh, I wonder what you people do with your lives
Oh, I wonder what you people do with your lives
Oh, I wonder what you people do with your lives
Oh, I wonder what you people do with your lives
Oh, I wonder what these people do with their lives
Oh, I wonder what these people do with their lives

When you find it, you'll feel it
I'll give you all of my love
Hold it, don't leave it, misuse it
As long as you believe enough

My mind is multiplying
I have so much to give
I won't underestimate you
For the way you feel that you want to live

Forever, forever
Forever, forever
Forever, forever

△

We decided to go ahead and record an album after Rob's death. It didn't have a title when we started working but I intended to write at least one song that would be massive – in terms of being emotionally far-reaching, rather than being a huge hit. A deeply personal song can connect and resonate with people. I wanted to go with a big title and there was nothing bigger than 'forever', a ubiquitous word, in this instance borrowed from the Wu-Tang Clan rather than the Spice Girls.

By the time I finished the lyrics for 'Forever' we had named the album *Us and Us Only*, a title that came from nowhere but summed up our post-Rob set-up; nine months in our own studio with no one else around. We were strangely without external expectations. There seemed to be no pressure from the record company, who possibly didn't want to appear insensitive.

In the middle of making the album we took a trip to Japan, where we were performing one gig in a five-day stay. The solitude and feelings of remoteness provided the perfect environment to attempt the big song I had in mind.

It was a contrast to what had become our new working life. Back home, *Tellin' Stories* had reached UK No. 1 and spawned a succession of big-selling, chart-bound singles. Our increased stature coincided with the rise of arenas in major cities. A tour required new elements including catering set-ups, separate trucks for lights, the occasional police escort and people working for us whose names we didn't know – all things that didn't sit comfortably with me. I'd always loved talking to fans and still do, but at that time we were on Saturday morning kids' TV and the glare of attention was overpowering at times. To be sitting in a hotel room in Japan with not much more than a pen and paper and the intention of writing a song was the perfect situation for me.

'Love is all there is' was something that had stuck in my mind after Rob died. Rob had a young daughter and some of the coverage of his passing had been negative. In some ways we'd lost everything and I returned to the basic building blocks that we started with. To build the Charlatans up again, we had to go back to the constant of the universe – we knew that everything could be constructed from love. But we also had to come out fighting.

For a long time, 'Forever' was the opening song of our live set. I hoped the audience didn't feel too awkward hearing me scream, 'Oh, I wonder what you people do with your lives?' I was reacting to what the tabloids had said about Rob's death, sensationalising what had happened. I was looking at it from the point of view of Rob's wife, Jo, and Emily, his daughter.

It would be similar when Jon Brookes became ill and died in 2013. The *Sun* printed a story about 'The curse of The Charlatans'. Yet over nearly thirty years, two of the band had died and the rest of us had been through various issues – we were just like any group of five ageing from their early twenties into their forties together. I thought of Debbie, Jon's wife, and their three children having to read those stories. Hack journalists became the target of my anger as nothing seemed to change in how insensitive they are as they eke out their living.

*Us and Us Only* described the way we felt then. We still get those feelings now – we have to remember what our band means to us, sometimes.

# 'MY BEAUTIFUL FRIEND'

*US AND US ONLY, 1999*

My beautiful friend
I will pay attention, don't say this is the end

I find it hard to describe you
To point and discover you
Could I tell you once again

Oh my beautiful friend

Let me sleep and I will feed you when you're hungry
Forever live inside of me
Through the holes in the pockets of my clothes

High, as high as an angel
I will stand there beside you
Love is all we need

Oh my, my, my beautiful friend
Oh my, my, my beautiful friend

My beautiful friend
I swear I adore you
Ain't no woman deep enough
I don't know how we made it this far dear
Without losing at least an ear

I could leave us, I could leave us a painting
Our lives are a-changing
Solid gold

I couldn't and I wouldn't evade you
Don't you know it, I can save, save you
I'll do it on my very own

Oh my, my, my beautiful friend
Oh my, my, my beautiful friend
My beautiful friend

Do you ever get this feeling
When it's hard to carry on

△

Being a songwriter means always having an outlet for your thoughts. When words go through a filter, it gives them a broader meaning and you find that there are links and connections that reach out around the world. So many people have said that the lyrics of 'My Beautiful Friend' have meant the most to them.

The song was written a short time after Rob died and we found that everything led us back to our beautiful friend. I didn't want to mention the loss itself because friendship isn't something that disappears. 'My Beautiful Friend' was about the other members of the band and the people around me as much as it was about Rob. When you lose someone you need everyone else even more. You're given the chance to cherish them and you're reminded not to take anyone for granted. It's a song I've always loved singing live – you get the feeling everyone has someone in mind when they hear it.

# 'IMPOSSIBLE'

*US AND US ONLY, 1999*

Impossible raw women, I know you're all too hard to please
I can help you if you only ask me kindly
Don't make me get down on my knees
God bless these hungry women, impossible to ever keep
Your breath has never tasted as sweet

I don't need you, to need me, to need my freedom
My freedom is a vision you seek
And the place you disappear to, is a place I wish to be
I beg you, instil you, don't treat it like some kind of joke
This song is, kind lady, my only hope

You can't kill an idea just 'cause it's raining
Keep it in the family, keep it in the kid
You know, they're handing out free tickets
This big old boat is a-startin' to sink

The whole world is getting hungry
And it ain't memories you need from me
And if memories are all you need from me
You're a hard act to please

I miss you and it's lonely, I admit, I can hardly sleep
You know he looks like a plastic surgeon
Just look at him, he's a piece
This whole world is like a postcard, easy lost and easy to reach
And if this is where you're going I will surely leave

Ex-impossible raw woman, you know you're oh so hard to please
Your new friend, he seems to love you
I hope he cries himself to sleep
She will fool you, destroy you, disappear without so much as smoke
This song is, cool lady, my only hope

I've always loved the arc of Bob Dylan's songs – his lyrics introduce you to a world that for a few minutes you inhabit alongside him. There is a sense of a landscape and a cinematic feel to them.

I've not tried to copy his style as such, which would obviously be easier said than done, but at this point I'd taken up playing the harmonica in a nod to the man and 'Impossible' was always going to start with a flourish of gob iron before the lyrics kicked in. The pronunciation of the first word is also a nod to Mr Zimmerman. But once underway, the lyrics cover jealousy, a failing relationship and hinted at what I thought might be happening to The Charlatans.

'Impossible, raw women/I know you're all too hard to please.' I saw myself as a raw person. Full of faults, imperfect, a product of my environment. I never wanted to settle down with anyone who made things easy for me. The girls I'd been attracted to all had an edge, and at that time a relationship I was in had just run aground. From a beautiful start we'd found ourselves in a place neither of us wanted to be and then I found myself dumped. I was young, I knew I'd bounce back, but it was tough at the time. And, yes, my replacement looked like a plastic surgeon. It's quite a cathartic song.

'She will fool you, destroy you, disappear without so much as a smoke/ This song is, cool lady, my only hope.' I had a feeling that anyone crossing paths with the girl that was now my ex, would suffer the same fate. As people we would all grow up and learn, and I'm happy to say that almost everyone lived happily ever after – although I can't speak for plastic-surgeon-guy. He disappeared . . . without so much as smoke.

'You know, they're handing out free tickets/This big old boat is a-startin' to sink.' The Charlatans were the boat and we felt like we were sinking after losing Rob. It was our first album without him and I felt the world had a ticket to watch us struggle.

The song sat on an eight-track portable studio in my flat. What happened next sounds like an episode in a cheesy biopic film that you never quite believe. Like some kind of showbiz soap opera, Tom and Ed of The Chemical Brothers had come over and I played them the song. Me and Ed were making cups of tea while Tom started doing what producers do, what singers might call 'tinkering'. Things were done to the piano, the drums were muted and then brought in with more focus. I had an effects rack, a Yamaha SPX 990 that was linked up to the eight-track, and magic was worked. Half a packet of biscuits later and 'Impossible' existed as it does on the album. When we play it now, none of the bitterness endures – it's gained some tenderness and it's a song I really love.

'Impossible' and 'Forever' are both song titles used by the Wu-Tang Clan. I wasn't aware of it being a conscious decision at the time, but they were the band I was listening to most. I found myself naturally drawing inspiration from their music.

# 'THE BLONDE WALTZ'

*US AND US ONLY, 1999*

Oh my love, my darling young son
All we need is a hungry council
Clean livin' it's all here in your home

Wouldn't it be nice to get away
Shout: 'Morning, how are you today?'
My hands are blazing
My arms are broken

I looked you up, I read your book
I held you up, I kept you good
I guess I didn't really take a look
I guess, I'm your man

Oh my love, be quiet and be quick
I found a house to live, keep out the weather
I'm blind and I'm sick

I heard the sound of thunder
In the place where all the poets sing
I couldn't get out, I couldn't get in
I'm hearing you, I'm hearing you

I looked up, I found love
I couldn't see I'll soon be thirty-three
I guess, I didn't really want to see
I guess, I'm your man

Oh lord, I feel my footsteps go on
All we need is a loving council clean living
And I'll keep moving on

I'll keep my guard and find another farm
Find a hospital to fix your broken arm
Be a pedigree on a higher ground
Come with me, come with me

Been run on, been walked on
Been spat upon, been whispered to
I guess I didn't mean to hurt you

I don't even try to think about it
Build yourself a ship and you destroy it
I always have to check to see if I'm still breathing

Oh my love, my darling young son
Go rest your weary head
I will pray for good to come

Wouldn't it be nice to get away
Shout: 'Morning, how are you today?'
My hands are blazing
My arms are broken

I took you up, I read your book
I looked you up, I kept you good
I guess I didn't really take a look
I guess, I'm your man
I guess, I'm your man

△

Until you start reading through a collection of lyrics, it's sometimes hard to notice themes, such as biblical motifs. In my songs, Jesus, Judas, angels, the Lord, the devil and the concept of holiness all feature.

I am more spiritual than I am religious, but there's a certain profundity that comes with biblical imagery. Much of songwriting for me is a search for higher powers (although once in a while it is necessary to cover subjects such as a dance craze that's sweeping through town/the world).

Sometimes the jumping-off point for lyrics can be the appreciation of songs by another artist. 'The Blonde Waltz' was inspired by Woody Guthrie, someone I'd only heard for the first time in 1998. Often I know the name of an artist but I've just never owned their records. I might discover them properly through the record collections of friends, on the radio or by reading about them in music magazines.

Martin Blunt is the subject of the song. He had become a single parent with two young kids and I was picturing them all making their way through life. I had a huge amount of respect for him and it was a real pleasure to see him being a fantastic dad: 'I held you up, I kept you good/I guess I didn't really take a look.' I was envisioning *The Lion King* with Martin's kids as little versions of Simba held up by their dad promising to protect them.

The first time we played this song was when we headlined the V98 festival. The ground had started to feel firm under our feet again. It was a year on from losing Rob and we'd decided we had to carry on and look to the future.

# 'SENSES (ANGEL ON MY SHOULDER)'

*US AND US ONLY, 1999*

You're my sweet black angel
Laughing on my shoulder
Always taking special care of me
You live with me in the night and in the day
And it's your world
You and me
You're an angel
You see only what you wish to see

Where's my sweet black angel
Laughing on my shoulder
Your world is my saviour
It's all that I live for
And it's your world
Oh it's your world
You live with me night and day
And you eat my whole heart away

Look at my skin shine
Look at my skin glow
Look at my skin laugh
Look at my skin cry

I'm tired of doing things for others
Who give nothing in return
Exchange a vow with my sweet angel
You're everything I do deserve
When you smile
Just a little bit
You're all I need
You and my philosophy

I am a simple messenger

I can help you if you please
I want you to be all I need to be, oh
Oh, to be what I need to be

△

The lyrics were written in our studio in Middlewich, a.k.a. the Big Mushroom.

During the making of *Us and Us Only*, producer Jim Spencer and I would concentrate on one area at a time – vocals, lyrics or melodies. Lyrics tended to be done on Sunday evenings, always one of my favourite times to write. By the tail end of the week the pressure is off and I'm in a place where I feel comfortable.

'Senses' is about the people I'd known and admired being part of my conscience and helping me in the future. A little bit like those rubber wristbands that say, 'What would Jesus do?' Except this is 'What would my sweet black angel do?' The lyrics describe an amalgamation of several different people whose influences I felt during the making of this record.

# 'JUDAS'

*WONDERLAND, 2001*

Searching for the very souls who've already been sold
Go on your way accordingly my son
I will privately accept you
And together sneak away and fly to another land

In the cold, cold eyes of Judas
Oh help me, in my hour of weakness
I will secretly accept you
And together we can fly away to another land

Ooh, can you tell me how you feel today
I found love, sweet, sweet music
Can you tell me how you feel today
I found love, sweet southern bliss
Yeah, yeah, yeah

Searching for the very souls who've already been sold
Go on your way accordingly my son
I will privately accept you
And together we can fly away to another land

In the cold, cold eyes of Judas
Oh help me, in my hour of weakness
I will secretly accept you
And together we can fly away to another land

Ooh, can you tell me how you feel today
I found love, sweet, sweet music
Can you tell me how you feel today
I found love, sweet southern bliss
Yeah, yeah, yeah

Ooh, can you tell me how you feel today
I found love, sweet, sweet music

Can you tell me how you feel today
I found love, sweet southern bliss
Yeah, yeah, yeah

△

Judas – a name with so much attached to it, from the biblical Judas to the famous accusation aimed at Bob Dylan when he went electric.

Biblical Judas is shunned after his betrayal of Jesus. He regrets his actions and ultimately kills himself.

You can become a victim of your own choices: it's a muddled world being in and around a band, characters come and go and the song was written with some of these characters in mind.

The antithesis of betrayal is loyalty and, in the end, I wanted this song to be about loyalty.

# 'YOU'RE SO PRETTY – WE'RE SO PRETTY'

*WONDERLAND, 2001*

Show me the diamonds
Show me the gold
Call me the answer, oh yeah
Call me anywhere
I don't have a care
This is my world

You're so pretty, we're so pretty

Show me the silver
Show me the gold
You're taking my name 'Angel'
Don't disappoint me
I see you smiling
Tie up my elbows, no joke

Talking to the Devil
Talking to the Lord
For one sweet touch
Talking me to Heaven
Talking me to Hell
For your sweet touch

You're so pretty, we're so pretty
You're so pretty, oh so pretty

(Show me the money
Show me the money, baby
Show me the money
Show me the money, baby

Show me the money
Show me the money, baby
Show me the money
Show me the money, baby)

You're so pretty, oh so pretty
You're so pretty, we're so pretty

All the hours
Asking questions
Couldn't fit in
Wasting time
Keep coming back
For a little more
I see you smiling

Feed me to the lions
I'll throw you to the floor
For one sweet touch
Diamonds in the rain
Will always be the same
When there's a rainbow

You're so pretty, we're so pretty
You're so pretty, oh so pretty

(Show me the money
Show me the money, baby
Show me the money
Show me the money, baby

Show me the money
Show me the money, baby
Show me the money
Show me the money, baby)

Oooh, oooh

I was listening to a lot of hip hop at the time of writing *Wonderland*, particularly ODB, Ol' Dirty Bastard, with 'Got Your Money' being a favourite. Admittedly, his lyrics veer into some scary territory, but I had money on my mind for the subject of a song.

'Show me the money' was a catchphrase of the time, transcending *Jerry Maguire* to adorn mugs and hats and become a cultural touchstone. It was the line the song was built around.

The title was inspired by a chapter in actor and comedian Steve Martin's book *Pure Drivel*, 'I Feel Pretty', that in turn came from a song title in *West Side Story*. It journeyed through my brain to become 'You're So Pretty – We're So Pretty'. I liked that it had a filmic quality and felt a little bit Hollywood.

We were recording in Los Angeles and my pronunciation of 'pretty' became Americanised, almost like a character singing my song. The track also shows the power of a few 'uh-uh-oohs' over actual words.

# 'A MAN NEEDS TO BE TOLD'

*WONDERLAND, 2001*

A man needs to be told there is a world going on
There is a world going on
There is a world going on

A man needs to be told to look into the light
He will get lost in the day
He will get lost in the night

A man needs to be told
A man needs to be told
A man needs to be told
A man needs to be told

A young boy once told me
I will be an old man and I am only fifteen
It wasn't part of the plan
It wasn't part of the dream

Ever wonder how much the man who wrote 'White Christmas' made
How evolution began
The revolution was fake

A man needs to be told . . .

A man needs to be told there is a war going on
There is a war going on
There is a war going on

Everyman needs to be told there is a truth in his eye
There is a rest in the dawn
There is a point to his life

A man needs to be told . . .

Paul McCartney and Keith Richards have both talked about songs coming to them in a dream. When you know that those songs are 'Yesterday', 'Let It Be' and the guitar riff from 'Satisfaction', it is enough to make any songwriter pay more attention to what happens after they fall asleep. Granted, not all dream songs work out – my masterpiece line, 'I'm at school, but I'm me now. And the teachers are all anteaters,' has yet to be recorded in anything but demo form.

The only lyrics that have ever come to me in a dream which we used were, 'A young boy once told me/I will be an old man and I'm only fifteen'. The next line, 'It wasn't part of the plan/It wasn't part of the dream,' refers to those words not being related to what I was dreaming about. They just kind of arrived. As I focused on them, the dream faded away, leaving only the words.

'A Man Needs to Be Told' was the song that was on the drawing board when the lyrics appeared. I got the title in Middlewich, while we were having a break in the pub during recording B-sides for *Us and Us Only*. I received an angry text that simply read, 'Sometimes, Tim Burgess, you need to be told'. The words 'A man needs to be told' swirled around my head and I needed to find a piano line to go with them. I ran the hundred yards back to the studio and asked Jim Spencer, our producer, to put a microphone on Tony's Challen piano. My playing is pretty basic, but the four notes I used with the phrase became the intro to the song.

Later, in Laurel Canyon, back home in Los Angeles, I was trying to pick my way through Bob Dylan's book *Tarantula*. It was quite heavy going too. At one point someone begs the question, 'I wonder how much the guy who wrote "White Christmas" made?'

# 'I BELIEVE IN THE SPIRIT'

*I BELIEVE*, 2003

I believe in the spirit
I believe in the holy ghost
I believe in the message
My message is my medium

I believe in all I stand up for
I believe in a get up for the poor
Ain't no emotional voice here for the choir
I know my faith will turn the flame into the fire

I believe in the city
I believe in the West Coast
I believe in no limit
I still believe in the miracles

I believe in California soul
I believe in everlasting love
Ain't no emotional voice here for the choir
I know my faith will turn the flame into the fire

You set the scene it's outta my hands
I believe in the woman, I believe in the man
Give up your ticket and pray for always
I'll give up mine and lead the parade

I need to get from East LA to join her
I need to get from Hollywood to Georgia
I need to get from East LA to join her
I need to get from Hollywood to Georgia

I believe in the spirit
I believe in the morning sun
I believe in you, silly
We all know just how good you are

I believe in a calm before a storm
I don't believe in pride before a fall
Ain't no emotional voice here for the choir
I know my faith will turn the flame into the fire

I need to get from East LA to join her
I need to get from Hollywood to Georgia
I need to get from East LA to join her
I need to get from Hollywood to Georgia

I believe in the spirit
I believe in the blue lamp
Jesus, and Jesus
Tell her to get from East LA to join us
I need to get from East LA to Georgia
I need to get from East LA to join her
I need to get from East LA to Georgia

△

When I lived in Hollywood the place was as much of a songwriting partner as any person I ever worked with, except Mark Collins.

David Lynch always credits the light in Los Angeles for being the perfect backdrop for a movie, but for me it was the atmosphere of the place that was beguiling. Material was never in short supply and Hollywood gets a credit on much of *Us and Us Only*, most of *You Cross My Path*, *Simpatico* and the lyrics for 'The Boxer' and all of *Wonderland* and my solo album *I Believe*.

I never felt like a stranger in Los Angeles, particularly as the Hollywood sign, the American accent and the temperament of the people are permanent fixtures on our TVs and cinema screens. But, more than that, I fell in love with the demeanour of almost everyone who works, serves and makes the place tick. I come from a country where a grumpy nod is all you might get when buying a drink, but in LA somebody will bounce up to say, 'How are you doing today? What can I get you? And you have yourself a nice day!' And I can vouch for this as, some days, pretty much all I did was order drinks. Some people say the transactions are fake but I take things at face value and if I am told to have a nice day, I will have a nice day. The city became a co-writer and the landscape provided all the melodies I needed.

In 2018, I headed back for a US tour with The Charlatans. It had been three years since my last visit and eight years since I gave up my residency. Returning was bittersweet. I had enjoyed such brilliant times and met some amazing people but by the end of that period for me it was time to go. It had become part of my history. At some point I'd love to go back again with my son and show him where I spent so much time before he arrived.

# 'OH MY CORAZON'

*I BELIEVE, 2003*

You are the spark that fuels my heart
Everything for us is written in the stars
But you're feeling used and so confused
Why do we do this to each other

I didn't mean to make you cry
Oh my corazon
I didn't mean to say goodbye
Oh my corazon
I didn't mean to hurt you

I have to leave you on your own
Back to the country where I once belonged
So adios mi corazon
I swear to bring my love back home now

I didn't mean to make you cry
Oh my corazon
I didn't mean to say goodbye
Oh my corazon
I didn't mean to hurt you

Moonlight on the patio
A kiss for a tear
Always giving me a sunrise
Help me through the fear
I will look into your life
Won't you leave with me tonight

I didn't mean to make you cry
Oh my corazon
I didn't mean to say goodbye
Oh my corazon
I didn't mean to make you cry

Oh my corazon
I didn't mean to say goodbye
Oh my corazon

I didn't mean to hurt you
I didn't mean to hurt you
I didn't mean to hurt you

△

There is a widescreen romance to Jack's Kerouac's *On the Road*, a book that has had a huge impact on me.

When he was talking about the Mexican Girl, as he called her, Kerouac was at his most lyrical. 'A pain stabbed my heart as it did every time I saw a girl I loved going the opposite direction in this world too big.' They travel from the streets of Los Angeles to the fields of the San Joaquin valley until the affair is over, fifteen pages later. I'd always wanted to capture that kind of feeling.

I first heard the word '*corazon*' ('heart' in Spanish) in the song 'Spanish Bombs' by The Clash – always a favourite. It was otherworldly, it told us The Clash were out in the wider world by the time *London Calling* was released in 1979.

I wrote the lyrics in the beautiful gardens at The Cat & Fiddle on Sunset Boulevard, next to the fountain, which I think it comes across in the song. It feels sunny whenever I get to sing it. The pub was owned by Kim and Paula Gardner. Kim was in the band The Creation, a fab, freakbeat combo from swinging '60s London. His daughter Eva played bass in my solo band. She also speaks Spanish, which helped me not make a fool out of myself. We still keep in touch. She plays bass for Pink and Cher, a polar opposite to the style of my live shows, but we remember them fondly.

# 'WE ALL NEED LOVE'

*I BELIEVE*, 2003

Teach me how to live
Teach me how to live without
There's only one thing I can't do without
Look at you and me now

Teach me how to live
I will teach you how to laugh
It's so very sad when people drift apart
And how they sometimes break your heart

We all need love
You and I
Whisper one sweet love
There we'll shine
I need to spend some time with you my love
I can't go on
I have to go on

Show me how to live
Show me how to live without
There's only one thing I believe I belong to
Look at you and me now

Teach me how to live
Teach me how to live without
It's so very sad when people drift apart
And how they sometimes break your heart

We all need love
You and I
Whisper one sweet love
There we'll shine
I need to spend some time with you my love
I can't go on

I have to go on

We all need love
You and I
Whisper one sweet love
There we'll shine
I need to spend some time with you my love
I can't go on
I have to go on

△

I felt I had a responsibility to The Charlatans and this fed into the way I wrote songs, but I took a different approach to my first solo album.

I wanted to write something that was outside of The Charlatans' sound. I'd never been a fan of boybands and their manufactured nature, but there was something about unashamed romance and stadium-sized sentiments that I liked. Pop lyrics are sometimes sneered at, but not by me. As much as I like what Crass are saying, I still really like the words to 'Never Forget' by Take That (suddenly I sound like I'm in group therapy: 'My name's Tim . . . and I like some boyband lyrics').

I was after something with vast appeal. Now, you might think I was going for the classic radio-friendly unit shifter and, in truth I was – but not for the cash. For me, it was more about the discipline of writing those kind of lyrics. It would turn out that 'We All Need Love' didn't become one of those aforementioned unit shifters, but I've since found out that it definitely means a lot to people.

Paul Weller played in Hollywood while I was living there and sent a message, asking if I would like to join him on stage for a song. I said, 'Yes,' and was getting anxious about which of his songs it would be. On the day he told me that he and his band had spent a couple of days learning,

'We All Need Love' – Paul Weller, a hero to me since I first started listening to music, had learnt one of my songs. A real moment in my songwriting life. I'd somehow never thought I was good enough, but Weller's seal of approval was something I cherished like a medal.

# 'YEARS AGO'

*I BELIEVE*, 2003

Do dodo do dodo do dodo do do
Do dodo do dodo do dodo do do

Years ago I used to feel my life was worth living
Do dodo do dodo do dodo do do
Years ago I used to feel that I could always fit in
Do dodo do dodo do dodo do do

Now I realise that there's a sadness in my soul
Now I realise I should've gone and walked right out the door

Years ago
Years ago
Years ago
Years ago

Do dodo do dodo do dodo do do
Do dodo do dodo do dodo do do

Years ago I used to feel that life was all about giving
Do dodo do dodo do dodo do do
Now I realise that everybody's always taking
Do dodo do dodo do dodo do do

I'm travelling down this chosen road that I ain't never been before
I'll walk alone and catch you later, I'll be back to
even up the score

From years ago
Years ago
Years ago
Years ago

Do dodo do dodo do dodo do do
Do dodo do dodo do dodo do do

I'd written some country-tinged bangers with Mark Collins and, as we were in the same band, all of them had up to this point ended up on Charlatans albums. 'Years Ago' had a different feel. It has a lightness to it lyrically and musically that wasn't where the band were at, but both of us really liked it.

We were on a short American tour in support of *Wonderland* when Mark came to my house in La Punta Drive in Hollywood. It was never lost on us that a kid from Salford (me) and a kid from Whalley Range (him) were drifting round film-set landscapes with guitars in hand. Cowboy hats were sometimes worn and the novelty and pure brilliance of our situation never left our smiling faces.

'Years Ago' is the only song co-written by Mark and me that wasn't released as a Charlatans' track.

# 'DEAD LOVE'

*UP AT THE LAKE, 2004*

How can you say love surrounds me
When you know it drowns me
Drowns me like you do

And you see
I am sitting for you
Waiting on you
Just like I do

How can you say love surrounds me and you
You kill me and break my poor heart up in two

It's dead love
Dead love
Dead love

How can you say love is in you
When you know you feel
Like the way you do

And you see
What you're doing to me
Take a chance now
I'll come to you

How can you say my life is like your own
When you break down in your own world I'll be gone

It's dead love
Dead love
Dead love

It's dead love
Dead love
Dead love

I was doing press for my first solo album and was feeling quite alone. This was mostly my own doing, although my relationship was breaking down and my connection with the band was at its most fragile.

I'd taken up with Carl Barat of The Libertines, who was in a similar spot, and together I think we made our feelings worse, albeit in a supportive way. I was the best part of fifteen years along the road with The Charlatans and he was seven years in – in Libertines years, which everybody knows is double a normal lifespan.

One of the great things about songwriting is that some of your strongest work comes when you're feeling unsure, so we took off for a few days to Paris and pen was put to paper. I told my partner 'Dead Love' was about the band and I told the band it was about my partner. Truth be told, 'Dead Love' was about me.

# 'FOR WHERE THERE IS LOVE THERE WILL ALWAYS BE MIRACLES'

'UP AT THE LAKE' B-SIDE, 2004

There is blood on my hands and there is fear in my eyes
For all greatness and freedom we can sail through the skies
You were the first and I gave you my word
For where there is love there will always be miracles

Where there is great love and great art there is great hope
I must be with the one that I love oh please let me go
You were the first and I gave you my word
For where there is love there will always be miracles

No thing to take care of we can just front, then we become
You wanted from me, you showed me your sheik, woke me up with your drum

Oh, come back to me we can straighten this out
We all have a bundle of front and a fistful of shout
You were the first and I gave you my word
For where there is love there will always be miracles

There is blood on my hands and there is fear in my eyes
For all sweetness and freedom we can dance through the skies
Yeah, you were the first and I gave you my word
For where there is love there will always be miracles

Yeah, for where there is love there will always be miracles
For where there is love there will always be miracles

I first visited Denver in 2002, when I was invited to a club night called Lip Gloss. There was a fantastic atmosphere in the club, inhabited by hipsters, dancers, straights, gays, indie kids, general party people and some who were all of the above.

I ended up playing the night twice, but on my first visit I was in a lyric-writing mood. I am not sure what the exact criteria for that is, but I recognise when the planets align and I get the familiar feelings of mild giddiness mixed with heightened trepidation. The resulting song ended up as a B-side, although my writing process makes no real distinction between a sure-fire Charlatans banger and a rarely heard, fan favourite B-side. Songs that are heard more often can feel ubiquitous, whereas others feel like buried treasure.

I landed in Denver loaded with hope, some great records and a feeling of positivity. I had written all the songs for my first solo album so there was no room at the inn for this new one. If the band liked it, it would be a Charlatans song. Reader, they loved it.

It was strange because my positivity was brought about by an overwhelming sense of negativity after a bust-up at home, but there is nothing like the open road, an airport and some time alone to get you looking around and seeing the best in things. I had been listening to Bob Dylan, whose song structures and delivery were guiding me through.

The line, 'Where there is great love and great art there is great hope,' came early and provides an anchor for the mood. Some of the imagery is very specific, such as the 'drum' in the line, 'You woke me up with your drum', which refers to the marching band of Hollywood High, whose rehearsals would invariably come pounding into my hangover dreams sometime in the late morning.

There was a mural opposite my apartment that depicted an Arab sheik with the words 'Hollywood High – sheik territory'. It struck me that it was meant to be a pun but I could never figure out what the pun was. The man in the mural always seemed to be looking at me judgementally, but maybe I needed judging at the time.

Anyway – back to Denver. I stayed for a couple of days and in that time the lyrics took shape. There was a bleakness to my life that was at odds with the uplifting music we were playing to the dancefloor. The music lifted me and allowed me to embrace positivity.

The title came first – which meant that there was only one way for the lyrics and the melody to go: 'For Where There is Love There Will Always Be Miracles', which landed in my head exactly like that. No explanation was needed as it left no doubt that, when you open up your heart, the possibilities are boundless (which would be a far less catchy title).

The song was eventually recorded in Bodmin, Devon, with Mark Collins, as a demo for potential inclusion on *Up at the Lake*. The positivity never quite propelled it to a home on the album but it ended up quite happily on the flip side of the seven-inch of the title track.

# 'TRY AGAIN TODAY'

*UP AT THE LAKE, 2004*

I don't know if I will always love you
I don't know if I will always need you
But I know that you'll find your own way tomorrow

I just hope I see you in the morning
I just hope I see you in this precious morning
And I know there is always the dream tomorrow

I'm going to try again today
To say what's in my heart
And pray for a better tomorrow
Make a brand new start
I'm telling everybody to turn it up again
Something's gotta change
Goodbye yesterday
Try again today
Something's gotta change

Maybe you can call me when you get to heaven
Maybe you should tell me I can go to hell
But I know rain or shine I'll be there tomorrow
Maybe it's written in the stars above you
Maybe it's just scratched out in the sand
But I know that you'll find your own dream tomorrow

I'm going to try again today
To say what's in my heart
And pray for a better tomorrow
Make a brand new start
I'm telling everybody to turn it up again
Something's gotta change
Goodbye yesterday
Try again today
Something's gotta change

I'm going to try again today
To say what's in my heart
And pray for a better tomorrow
Make a brand new start
I'm telling everybody to turn it up again
Something's gotta change
Goodbye yesterday
Try again today
Something's gotta change

△

Some song lyrics can put a spring in your step and I'm not just talking about saccharine sweet words.

I love a song that can lift my spirits but that is realistic too. For me, 'God Only Knows' by The Beach Boys is a song that manages to do this. It starts with 'I may not always love you', which is perhaps not the best opener for a love song. I didn't have their song consciously in my mind when writing 'Try Again Today' and genuinely only realised it when it came to writing this book, but that's the way of the universe sometimes.

I wanted to write something that would come to mind when you have to dig deep. When things are not going that well. Big anthems are good, but this ended up as a small album. It's not about climbing the highest mountain, it's just about having another go, not setting your expectations too high. The lyrics are quite sparse. Lots of people say it's a song that has helped them out in tough times and because of that I'm really proud of it.

# 'BLACKENED BLUE EYES'

*SIMPATICO, 2006*

A charlatan, I
Noble and wild
Hustling for tricks to help you feel loved
And we all need a shoulder to cry on
Once in a while
And there won't be a dry eye
In the house tonight

Blackened blue eyes
I don't care too much for your
Circumstances or you
Situation-wise

A charlatan, I
Will blossom and die
One day you'll find a real need for love
Or you live with the fear
For the rest of your life
And there won't be a dry eye
In the house tonight

Blackened blue eyes
I don't care too much for your
Circumstances or you
Situation-wise

The one thing I hate
The numb and the fake
The gutless who rape
The jaws of a snake
We all need a best friend
We can trust with our lives till the end
And there won't be a dry eye
In the house tonight

144

Blackened blue eyes
I don't care too much for
Second chances
Blackened blue eyes
I don't care too much for
Final chances

Ride out into a world of random prostitutes
I'll show you some fantastic scenes
And it will be alright

Blackened blue eyes
Blackened blue eyes
Blackened blue eyes
Blackened blue eyes
Blackened blue eyes

△

When we handed *Simpatico* to the label, the powers that be furrowed their brows and decided that 'Blackened Blue Eyes' would be the single. I didn't think the lyrics were as good as they could be and asked if they could give me a day to rewrite it. I don't recall the original words exactly, but they didn't include the opening lines as you might know them.

The song is about an actual person, a friend pushed around a little too much by the world. I hadn't myself been best placed to give her advice at the time and so I wrote the song and played it to her. Something seemed to dawn on us simultaneously. In a short space of time we'd levelled out from mini-nose dives and we both gave the song some credit for working on us subconsciously.

The opening lines were still not what I wanted them to be. As in a buddy-cop movie, I was given twenty-four hours to fix the song before it was sent to the pressing plant. Pressure to hit a deadline was not something I was fond of, but in this instance it was the perfect push that I needed to write the song.

I always liked when bands referenced themselves by name – 'A Charlatan I noble and wild' had something of Adam and the Ants and sounded like the opening line to a novel. 'Hustling for tricks' is a bit wild west, and at the time I was feeling out in the wilderness. 'And there won't be a dry eye/In the house tonight' has a theatrical feel.

I had a photograph of Joe Strummer lying on the floor writing lyrics around the time *London Calling* was released and I've always wondered what the song was that he was writing. I felt a thrill looking at it, as if the rest of The Clash might be in another part of the studio waiting for his words, and 'Blackened Blue Eyes' was my own version of that picture.

# 'FOR YOUR ENTERTAINMENT'

*SIMPATICO, 2006*

Try not to die
Try not to die
Hold me tight
I know there's something going wrong inside

Tonight tonight
The stars are bright
Watch me close
Because I'm looking for the last laugh

For your entertainment
For your entertainment
For your entertainment
For your entertainment

I know you lie
I know you lie
Looking for the boys
With the needles in their eyes

Hold me close
For the first kiss
I guess I'm looking
For something that just don't exist

For your entertainment . . .

The title might suggest a jolly number, but the opening lines of the song put paid to that: 'Try not to die/Try not to die.'

The song was built around feeling as if I was just there for everyone else's entertainment. I had my role in the band, but I felt like much of everything else had been stripped away. My emotions were in large part triggered by my increased intake of drugs – over the counter . . . under the counter . . . round the back of the shop, and whatever you've got. Drug use heightened my sense of self-pity, in turn making me believe I was there for everyone else's entertainment when, in fact, I am pretty sure I wasn't entertaining anyone at all. Sorry if you've just opened the book at this page – there's more cheery stuff on the other pages.

Looking back, I can see that I was trying to tell myself to get my act together while there was still an act for me to be a part of. I know that singers are prone to dramatic outbursts, but years have passed and many of my closest friends have since confided in me that they were really worried for me. Yet, as many of us know, if you point these things out to someone in the middle of their difficulties, you may end up just being rejected.

Tonight tonight
The stars are bright
Watch me close
Because I'm looking for the last laugh

In that condition your mind plays tricks on you and mine was telling me that the ultimate piece of entertainment could be checking out completely – yeah, like I said, we singers can be prone to dramatic statements.

Hold me close
For the first kiss
I guess I'm looking
For something that just don't exist

The thing that I didn't think existed was a way out. My bandmates had always been my best friends but it felt like even they were at the end of their tether.

# 'THE ARCHITECT'

*SIMPATICO, 2006*

Rockers all over the world reunite
In love with the feeling that comes with the night
As we talk
Lay off the pills that are left on the shelf
We'll be warped when we stop

I never said I want to be the one who said
I told you so
But you're all a lowly bunch of parasites
And I told my girl that it would be alright
Let me go

On a hilltop in the bustley nights
With a legendary lord I used to like
And there will be tears in our eyes

Make love in our own little van
I am giving you all that I can, and I am
Buckle my belt and I roll up the sleeves of my shirt
And I flirt

I never said I want to be the one who said
I told you so
But you're all a lowly bunch of parasites
And I told my girl that it would be alright
Let me go

On a hilltop in the bustley nights
With a legendary lord I used to like
And there will be tears in our eyes

I never said I want to be the one who said
I told you so
But you're all a lowly bunch of parasites

And I told my girl that it would be alright
Let me go

On a hilltop in the bustley nights
With the legendary lords I never liked
And there will be tears in our eyes

Last night you know an architect saved my life
I knew in my heart that I would die tonight
I knew in my heart I wouldn't die tonight

Thank you all
I thank you all so very very very much
You know I never really wanted to be touched
Oh, to be touched
Oh, to be touched

△

We'd been working with Dean Fragile, who fulfilled the roles of tour DJ, friendly face and counsellor. He had a photo on MySpace and for some reason I'd written 'the architect' on a copy of the photo. It sat there for a while and it was almost like I'd left myself a subliminal message for a song title. I set about getting some words together.

Rockers all over the world reunite
In love with the feeling that comes with the night
As we talk
Lay off the pills that are left on the shelf
We'll be warped when we stop

This was me in another dimension talking to me in the real world. I'm usually the first person to try to figure out what my lyrics mean and to be totally truthful I am not sure I really know sometimes.

> I never said I want to be the one who said
> I told you so
> But you're all a lowly bunch of parasites
> And I told my girl that it would be alright
> Let me go

> On a hilltop in the bustley nights
> With a legendary lord I used to like
> And there will be tears in our eyes

We were a group of friends who were falling out with each other and the band was falling apart. We had producer and musician Trevor Horn's studio booked, but I was in a rut. The more I tried to figure my way out, the more tangled I became – I felt that Dean could show me the way out of the maze.

> Buckle my belt and I roll up the sleeves of my shirt
> And I flirt

'Rolling up my sleeves' and 'buckling my belt' were things my dad used to say about needing to concentrate, getting stuck into a job. I see *Simpatico* as a transition – the last album on which I would be bogged down by the demons that were getting the better of me.

> Last night you know an architect saved my life
> I knew in my heart that I would die tonight
> I knew in my heart I wouldn't die tonight

Everything about *Simpatico* was dark – the artwork, the lyrics, the headspace, the working relationships; we seemed to be setting each other up for failure. But the last two lines of the song form the point at which the light comes in.

In 2008, Mark and Tony Rogers rented an apartment on Hollywood and Vine, Los Angeles. Ten years later, on the day of our show at the Teregram in the same city, I walked past their former lobby entrance on the opposite side of the road and it seemed like we had only been recording yesterday. I could see them bowling out of the front door, full of the enthusiasm that we had had when we started *Simpatico*. Two worlds collided and I was existing both then and now. I took the red line up to the NoHo district and wandered around my old haunts – Gelson's, my favourite supermarket in the world, the creepy, *Addams Family*-esque, mock Bavarian castle of the Scientology building and the glare and the sprinklers of Los Feliz, with the smell of jasmine.

It was a hypnotic, multisensory overload that took me back to both the last time and the first time I was there. I went past the 101 Coffee Shop, the coolest diner imaginable, and it felt like 2000 again. I could hear the whoops of delight from Mark Collins and his family as they moved out of Chorlton, Manchester, and took up residence over the road from me in the Hollywood Dell.

Living the dream is a phrase that has become cliched through overuse but I knew it then and I know it now – that was exactly what we were doing.

# 'OH! VANITY'

*YOU CROSS MY PATH, 2008*

When I was a little child
What you'd call a runaway
Find me with a latch and key
Crawling in the dirt

There's a problem just for me
I have a thousand words to sing
Always one for running wild
And dressing up to be like you

Oh vanity, oh vanity
Will keep me from insanity
This heart of mine would rather die
Than live a lie for humanity

And now I'm all grown up to be
A paranoid schizophrenic
My friends are all like me and you
I can't tell 'em what to do

There's another world to see
Lie down with dogs and you'll get fleas
When Paris gave her hand to me
It felt like an eternity

Now as I feel I'm growing up
It's like a drug
It's like a drug

Oh promise me, oh promise me
You'll save the one last dance for me

Oh promise me, oh promise me
You'll save the one last dance for me

Oh promise me, oh promise me
You'll save the one last dance for me

Oh vanity, oh vanity
You'll save the one last dance for me

Oh promise me, oh promise me
You'll save the one last dance for me

Oh promise me, oh promise me
You'll save the one last dance for me

△

I know some songwriters who agree that the process of writing is like being a satellite dish. You take in signals from all over and your song ends up as the TV set through which you broadcast. You sift out the white noise, static and bad ideas before showtime.

Inspiration can come when I'm wandering lonely as a cloud, but other times it arrives amid the hubbub of a showbiz party in West Hollywood. To set this particular scene, it was being held by William Morris, powerhouse agents extraordinaire, who are a part of the fabric of Tinseltown itself.

Queens of the Stone Age's Josh Homme was present and I counted at least two Wilsons (neither one was Owen), Courtney Love, Jacks White and Black, lots of the box-set glitterati and somewhere, after the A-list, the names of T. Rogers, M. Collins and T. Burgess, esq.

We were glad-handed by staff and cocktail waiters on arrival. It was the kind of party at which hot dogs were served with vintage champagne and there was a permanent queue for the toilets with occupants in pairs. I had given up everything by then – including hotdogs – but there was something about those parties that I could enjoy in any state. And my newfound sobriety meant it was easier to get home by midnight as opposed to two days later.

One of my friends was an agent who looked after Queens of the Stone Age, Eminem and Coldplay. Far from home, he was originally from Northern Ireland, and at one point said, 'I have got someone I want to introduce you to, someone who I think you'll like.' I was secretly hoping that he was referring to Prince, walking past me on his way in, surrounded by bouncers in white tuxedos.

The next minute a hand was thrust my way with its owner exclaiming, 'Hi, I am Paris!' There was no need for a surname as at that time Paris Hilton seemed to be on every magazine cover, news channel and supermarket tabloid. She made an immediate impression and, although the world was then judging her, I thought she was cool. She had to be strong to stay standing. Was she talented? Well, was anyone in that room talented? Actually, Prince was there so, yeah, but it's a more philosophical point I'm trying to make here as well as explain two lines of 'Oh! Vanity':

When Paris gave her hand to me
It felt like an eternity

# 'YOU CROSS MY PATH'

*YOU CROSS MY PATH, 2008*

I don't think you quite know who I am
I am the son of loyalty
I hope you understand
I don't think you quite know who I am
Oh, I am the sum of everything
I don't want you to understand

You cross my path, I'll take you down
You bloodied me with howling hands
The wretched games, the tortured souls
The flowing scarves of debutantes
The crushing blows, the sordid scenes
But what you did was so obscene

I will ride again
And I'll take you down like that
You will die up there alone
I'll take you down like that

You think about me every day
You dream of ways to keep your evil thoughts at bay
You think about me every day
You dream of ways to keep your sicko thoughts at bay

You cross my path, I'll take you down
You bloodied me with howling hands
The wretched games, the tortured souls
The flowing scarves of debutantes
The crushing blows, the sordid scenes
But what you did was so obscene

I will ride again
And I'll take you down like that
You will die up there alone
I'll take you down like that

I will sail into your kingdom
Be the sound of the abyss
Could be the sound of your own voice
Be the sound of your first kiss
I am the sound of Iraq
I am the sound of the Red Sea
I am the force of the almighty
I am the sound of your own dreams

You cross my path, I'll take you down
You bloodied me with howling hands
The wretched games, the tortured souls
The flowing scarves of debutantes
The crushing blows, the sordid scenes
But what you did was so obscene

I will ride again
And I'll take you down like that
You will die up there alone
I'll take you down like that

I will die for no one
I will cry for no one
You will die up there alone
You will die up there alone

I'll get you, I'll get you . . .

Every lyricist needs tools to write their next masterpiece and I needed a bath, 'Sunrise' by New Order, 'Anti-Fade' by Chrome and 'Circus of Death' by the Human League. All of those songs hold huge importance for me.

Bob Dylan only needed a few chords to get his message across and, while the choice of those chords may seem insignificant to the listener, I presume they were of the utmost importance to him. It was the flow and roll of line after line of lyrical brilliance that the world lapped up, although I wouldn't say the music of 'You Cross My Path' is insignificant.

Some lyrics conjure a mood and the subject can be hard to figure out, but these songs fit around the listener. The lyrics to 'You Cross My Path', though, are plain and simple. The protagonist – who we can call me – is angry at someone and has notions of hatred and revenge. It's a magnified view of a situation, taken in shorthand, but songs don't have long to deal with their subject and I grew up listening to music that was fuelled by frustration and anger.

The subject of the song is an amalgamation of a couple of people who had crossed the band and it was a letter to them. I was showing facets of myself that I don't often reveal and I think of it in the same way that an author might have a character who expresses their views. The business side of the music industry has a few unsavoury characters and this song is a handy shot across their bows.

There was a catharsis to writing a song like 'You Cross My Path' – it felt almost like therapy. I dealt with my feelings and left them on the paper. It's one I like performing live as it's a good way to let off some steam.

# 'MY NAME IS DESPAIR'

*YOU CROSS MY PATH, 2008*

In the swell
In the swim
You miss my stare

In the square
Take my hand
My own cross to bear

You miss my stare
My name is despair

Save your soul
Save your soul
A path that I once shared

Could my presence
Be too much

You will miss my stare
My name is despair

You miss my stare
My name is despair

Slightly worn
Incomplete
I was lost
Incomplete

Slightly marred
Through defeat
In a vacuum
Incomplete

My only prayer
My name is despair

You will miss my stare
My name is despair

My name is despair
My name is despair

My only prayer
My name is despair


# 'BIRD'

*YOU CROSS MY PATH, 2008*

I wish I could die

In your arms tonight

There's part of me leaving

Believing the hype

I wish I was a bird

Wouldn't that be absurd

To flap at your window

To breathe you the word

# 'THIS IS THE END'

*YOU CROSS MY PATH, 2008*

This is the end
I'll take a bow
With one reprise

Where I come from I don't see the sun
With friends I fold

I wander lonely as a cloud
Oh
'Cause I did it my way

I look beyond the cuts and I see
Through the scars
This is the end

This is the end of all I know
Can't let you tell me what to do
Oh I will never be put down

Oh I will never be put down
Oh I will only be set free
This is the end for you and me

This is the end
I'll say goodbye
The final curtain

I look at all the amputees on the strip
And think this is the end

This is the end of all I know
Can't let you tell me what to do
Oh I will never be put down

Oh I will never be put down
Oh I will only be set free
This is the end for you and me

This is the end
I'll take a bow
With one last reprise

$\triangle$

If I were more proggy I might refer to these three songs as a suite. When I was growing up tracks that fit together had been quite a thing in prog.

The title of 'My Name is Despair' came first and felt like the name of a pulp novel or a vengeful western. It had atmosphere and that was a good place to start. I wanted to evoke a Sergio Leone-style movie – the original idea for the name of the album was *The Gothic Wild West*, but as with most records, things moved.

I had a feeling that everything was going to change for me. I was leaving an old life behind. I felt my previous existence was like a sea in which I was caught in the swell. There was a vacuum I had to move into and I didn't know the rules or even if I would be able to cope. My feelings were of excitement but I felt as if despair was perhaps waiting for me. Everything was ready to be introduced and take me on another ride.

The three songs were all written within a two-week period. 'This is the End' came first, followed by 'My Name is Despair'; 'BIRD' was the final piece of the puzzle. From the story of Noah's Ark to the work of Edgar Allan Poe, birds are seen as messengers. 'BIRD' is about a bird at a window trying to deliver a message. I was anxious in case the future wouldn't work out for me. I started to question whether my best days were behind me. Doubts are the curse and the muse of a songwriter. Cheerful ditties are all well and good but songs inspired by angst and the unknown seem to chime best with our audience. I always used to wonder how singers continued to write great lyrics after becoming comfortable, but I've now realised that their horizons become broader. Bruce Springsteen is as gritty in his world view, despite being able to buy numerous cars for an infinite number of garages.

Whenever I wrote down 'BIRD' as a title, I'd always write it in capital letters. It's a nod to David Lynch – a tiny detail that I've never really mentioned as it's not immediately obvious as a reference. He used upper case on the credits and artwork for his film *Inland Empire*. I suppose here is as good as anywhere to mention that rather oblique fact.

There is a superstitious element to this three-card song trick that fits with the album artwork, a series of sketches of a black cat by Faris Badwan from The Horrors. The songs deal with the end but, like the death card for a tarot reader, it represents a huge change more than the cue to shuffle off this mortal coil. One thing is left behind and something else starts. It's tempting to dwell on the old when you are leaving.

# 'LOVE IS ENDING'

*WHO WE TOUCH*, 2010

Sleep like a child with no pillow
Eyes open looking for a smile
And when I see tomorrow
Cupid comes out for a while

Promises whisper like vapour
Float inside like an empty lie
Your words flutter like paper
In the skies I say goodbye

Stop pretending
Love is ending
Am I trying
Day after day, you make me feel this way

Sweet dreams gently descending
Felt your hair float across my skin
Sleep soft after the kissing
Free the soul undo the pin
What did you say you'd do for me
I want to pick you up
And if you need to see through me
You just have to take a look

Stop pretending
Love is ending
Am I trying
Day after day, you make me feel this way
Oh day after day, you make me feel this way

Stop pretending
Love is ending
Not possessing
Am I trying

THE ROOTS & WINGS

Stop pretending
Love is ending
Not possessing
I am trying

Stop pretending
Love is ending
Am I trying
Day after day, you make me feel this way

Stop pretending
Love is ending
Am I trying
Day after day, you make me feel this way
Oh after day, you make me feel this way

△

More endings, although it was a beginning of a new life for me.

Many of the lyrics were written in a stream-of-consciousness style, revealing themselves as they were being written. 'Love is ending' was a mantra going round in my head but I didn't know where it was coming from. It could have been about the band or living in Los Angeles but, as it transpired, it was much more literal. Shortly after writing the song I left my life as part of a couple and moved alone back to London.

# 'THE DOORS OF THEN'

*OH NO I LOVE YOU, 2012*

Time be deranged
Devout and pure
The oddest frame of sense
Both steadfast and demure
We do

Oh no I love you
Hello I love you

One of the girls
None of the flowers
A kiss, the wine, the thanks
We took each other's hand below

Oh no I love you
Hello I love you

Behind the doors of then
Remembering the where and when

Oh no I love you
Hello I love you

Lyric writing is often a solitary affair, while the recording process may introduce outside influences. When lines are clunky – just not right – Martin, or at one time Rob, and sometimes Mark would make a suggestion. I am not sure how it works with other musicians, but did Lennon and McCartney write absolutely every one of those words or should some of the songs be credited to 'Lennon/McCartney and McCartney's mate Steve' or to 'Lennon/McCartney and Lennon's auntie's friend'?

I went to Kurt Wagner from Lambchop to work on an album that became *Oh No I Love You*. We came up with a format that we both liked: I would write the music and he the lyrics. Ideas worked backwards and forwards and so, of course, it was a bit more complex than that. I came up with broad brushstrokes of lyrics that Kurt would use as a guide, keeping or discarding depending on his view of their shape.

Cheekily, I presented this song as 'Hello, I Love You'. It duly came back as 'The Doors of Then'. I'm guessing he got 'The Doors' element from the song title I 'borrowed' from the band (which in turn comes from Aldous Huxley's 1954 book *The Doors of Perception*) and the song became a runaway train from there.

# 'EMILIE'

*MODERN NATURE, 2015*

Honesty
Is no mistake
Pretty girls
Just make waves
And together
You could say that we are a team
Living the dream

Would you call
I fell asleep
Better not
Tell them the truth
For Emilie
Lives in a made up place
She doesn't need to escape

There is no need to look for me
I am looking through you
There is no need to look for me
Emilie

Emilie
Just in case
I miss you pass
This way again
Only I
Know what this means to me
And how this could be

There is no need to ask for me
I am asking for you
There is no need to ask for me
Honestly

Emilie
Emilie

A perk of the success of The Charlatans is that songs can be hothoused if need be. Nothing too extravagant, but a short holiday or some dedicated time in the right environment often results in a gem.

One such trip took place around 2012, to a cottage by the sea near Dungeness – it's not all glamour – which was out of season. Much of the local area was closed. Mark and I gathered supplies from nearby Hastings and took to our accommodation. I've always quite liked the idea of a post-heist hideout that makes for a tense but open landscape. I can imagine the mix of shady characters passing time, their sole intention not to be tracked down. They don't want to let the pressure get to them. It was the same for us – in a situation that was partly *In Bruges*, with a touch of *Reservoir Dogs*, we were tasked with coming back with plenty of ideas, if not completed songs.

Mark had a guitar riff that brought to mind the glory days of The Kinks and I wanted to find something cinematic. I had in mind something between *Wuthering Heights* and *The French Lieutenant's Woman* and the lyrics in my head were 'Do You Know the Way to San Jose'.

The initial idea was for the song to be a letter to the fictitious Emilie, a story that was never quite clear. It was a snapshot of a tale that had somehow gone wrong in the mind of the storyteller.

As part of Record Store Day celebrations, we loaned Laura Cantrell the music in the form of a dramatic string arrangement by Sean O'Hagen. Laura perpetuated the literary feel by sending us Emilie's 'reply', naming the original song's protagonist 'Emanuel' in her lyrics. It was a bizarre but interesting idea, allowing her to continue the story as in those drawings you did when you're a kid, drawing part of a monster, folding it over and passing it to someone else to finish.

Everyone did those, right?

# 'TALKING IN TONES'

*MODERN NATURE, 2015*

I never liked the fact
And I don't like to moan
I thought we had a pact

Talking in tones

I don't know how to act
When you pick up the phone
I'll start filling in the gaps

Talking in tones
Talking in tones

Ooh I feel strengthened by your presence
Ooh it's like heaven, in sixes and sevens

I never liked the fact
And I don't like to moan
Just keeping us on track

Talking in tones
Talking in tones

Ooh I feel strengthened by your presence
Ooh it's like heaven, in sixes and sevens
Ooh I feel strengthened by your presence

It's like heaven
It's like heaven
It's like heaven

This song began with the title and with the title came the subject. I wanted it to be about the subliminal communication between two people who really understand each other, whether they are engaged in a project, living together or just have a connection.

It was written in 2011, when riots were breaking out in cities around the UK. The unrest seemed to be subliminally communicated, predicted and then became a self-fulfilling prophecy. The weirdest of times.

R Stevie Moore was over from Nashville to play a series of dates, but his Manchester show was cancelled as looters and rioters were expected around the venue. I'd made a special trip to see him and had a couple of unexpected days with nobody around and nothing to do. I took that time to write lyrics to what would become 'A Gain' and 'Talking in Tones', both accompanied by rudimentary chords on acoustic guitar, and melodies, the latter played over the beat from 'Love to Love You Baby'. I sent both songs to Kurt Wagner to look over. He took on 'A Gain' but when I showed the same words to The Charlatans we decided that 'Talking in Tones' would fit with the style we were after for *Modern Nature*. Before long we had something we were all happy with.

# 'SO OH'

*MODERN NATURE, 2015*

So Oh
So Oh
Oh Oh

Some other night
And I'm lying on my back
Looking up
And I can't see the stars for the trees
And I'm sitting now, thinking
Just wondering where I've been

So Oh
So Oh
Oh Oh

So Oh
So Oh
Oh Oh

I watch from my seat
And I thought I saw the lights
Through the clouds I caught the sunset
The world just might have changed

Following the lines of latitude
I hit the ground
Just landed

Following ascension gaining altitude
I'm sitting in a tin can, just to find you

So Oh
So Oh
In love

City lights (So Oh)
You and me
And the free (So Oh)
Summary

On a high (So Oh)
Walking to certain bliss (So Oh)
Summer

△

At times you can write the lyrics that express the opposite of what you're feeling – or at least that's how it works with me. I find it easy to come up with a cheerful song when I am a little bit down in the dumps and if I am happy my mind turns to more depressing thoughts.

A breezy sunshine song is best undertaken in freezing conditions. 'So Oh' was written in snowy Middlewich, but the sunshiney lyrics paid off when the record company decided that a beautiful sunny beach near Rome would be the best place to film a video.

I had written something that was just, 'Oh so ... something.' I am not sure what it was now, but I looked at the two-letter words and thought they would sound good flipped around. If the words aren't what might regularly be used then you have to have a killer melody, as I was to discover when I had to put a few verses together.

I was in a contemplative state, away from family, near where I grew up, so I was an antenna for positive vibes. There was a little bit of *The Man Who Fell to Earth* and it was quite a new life for me – singers are often the centre of attention, by accident or design, and life on tour and in a band can make you feel a little selfish. But by then I had a toddler who was relying on me and was starting to recognise me and I could feel a whole new world opening up for both of us.

The trip for the video was done at a time when I was the lead parent so it was pretty much our first road trip together. We ended up hiring a little car for the video and the shoot took place on a beach. It made me realise how lucky I am and whenever I sing this song I am transported back to that beach.

# 'COME HOME BABY'

*MODERN NATURE, 2015*

Joy, it's such a joy
Watching the smile on your face
You're looking up at my face

We are working it through
A solution for you and for me
Nothing between
What will be

Come home baby
Come home baby
Kiss me gently
I can't wait
Don't hesitate
Let's be together

Words can mean many things
Watching you step in time
Leaving the bad days behind

No one can take your place
Maybe I'm out of step
Maybe I'm out of my depth

Come home baby
Come home baby
Kiss me gently
I can't wait
Don't hesitate
Let's be together

I can't wait
No one can take your place
Maybe I'm out my depth

Come home baby
Come home baby
Come home baby

I can't wait
And celebrate
Us being together

I can't wait
Can't wait

△

I had Jon Brookes' wife Debbie in mind when I wrote these lyrics. Tony had already done most of the music and it sounded fantastic. I wanted to give it words that befit the scale. Some inspiration walks a bizarre path and the title of this has one such backstory.

Newsreader and war correspondent Martin Geissler could never be fully sure if he was coming back from travelling to danger zones; it was an occupational hazard. He once drove back from an airport listening to 'Just When You're Thinking Things Over' and he said that hearing the words coming home was part of the process of celebrating the basic feeling of being alive. The power of his description has never left me and the feelings of coming home or wanting someone else to come home stuck in a loop in my head.

When I heard what Tony had sent there was a phrase for four syllables in what seemed to be the chorus. By the second listen, 'Come home baby' had made its way into the song. I had lost Jon and had become a dad for the first time. Before his death we would discuss the impending change in my role – he was a dad of three and had endless advice and stories. The song is a celebration of the connection between people.

# 'TROUBLE UNDERSTANDING'

*MODERN NATURE, 2015*

Another day
Keeping it familiar
Love you baby
Another hour no interruption

We need to be held to be aware of our own bodies
Nature is
Trouble understanding

Another minute
And it could be a different ending
Another second and it's gone

Sometimes you're up for breakfast on a clear day
Nature is
Trouble understanding

We need to be held to be aware of our own bodies
Nature is
Trouble understanding

We need to be held to be aware of our own bodies
Nature is
Trouble understanding

We need to be held to be aware of our own bodies
Nature is
Trouble understanding

While I was coming to terms with Jon's death, Nik, my partner, was away on tour. Morgan, our son, was a few months old. News came in that Lou Reed had died.

Thinking about the idea of the cycle of life, I was sitting in the kitchen at home staring out of the window at a tree. It was autumn. It came to me that I'd had my lifetime to deal with the idea of losing people, grieving and navigating life's complexities but it would soon be my task to explain as best I could these ideas to my son. The phrase, 'Trouble understanding' stuck with me. It was something I'd experienced and I imagine everybody has the same difficulties with the big things in life. You realise as you get older that your younger self did well to cope and that nobody necessarily has any more of a clue than anyone else. Parenting teaches you that.

I feel that we all walk around, especially while grieving, being numb to our physical form. Human contact reminds us of what we are and allows us to reconnect. 'We need to be held to be aware of our own bodies'

At first, I thought it was a song that would become part of the album I was writing with Peter Gordon but as the lyrics came together I realised it was a Charlatans song.

It was a real honour when Sharon Horgan said how much she loved the song and asked if it could be used in an episode of *Catastrophe*.

# 'KEEP ENOUGH'

*MODERN NATURE, 2015*

My affection is moving
I have the old in my hand
Tempt me to agree
I'm a sensitive man

Is this the beginning
'Cause it feels like the start
Remember where you were
Yesterday

Keep it up
Keep it up
Keep it up

Today I am new
The direction is key
In you is the answer
Soon-to-be

My thoughts tend to linger
Oh friend of mine
Affections run deeper
Keep it up

Keep it up
Keep it up
Keep it up

Finding it hard
Keeping up
Have to make sure
We keep enough

My affection is moving
I have the old in my hand
Tempt me to agree
I'm a sensitive man


Is this the beginning
'Cause it feels like the start
Remember where you were
Yesterday


Keep it up
Keep it up
Keep it up
Keep it up
Keep it up


△

We had tried to write songs while Jon was ill but, as we moved towards the inevitable, we ceased to function. Jon died and we dealt with our grief, but we didn't know if the band would continue; we were mourning our friend with little heed to what we would do afterwards. We played at the Royal Albert Hall in celebration of his life and then we had a decision to make – at least, in some ways it was ours. In others, it was out of our hands. If the songs didn't come then it was obvious that we had reached our conclusion.

'Keep Enough' was the first song we wrote after Jon died. We wanted to go for a soulful song in the vein of Curtis Mayfield or even Barry White. 'Keep it up', those actual words, came first. Doing what we'd always done was what we needed to do. Rather than try to start anything too new we first had to become a band again.

I knew the words would be sparse but there was a clear message – 'Is this the beginning/'Cause it feels like the start.' Jon wouldn't have wanted his death to be the end, but just a change, a new beginning. It's all in there. We were finding it hard, we had to make sure we were doing the right thing – the direction we went in was key.

The result was a song we felt that Jon would have loved. We'd become a band again and we took the small steps that then led to more songs that would end up as *Modern Nature*.

# 'LOT TO SAY'

*MODERN NATURE, 2015*

If I could

Have anything

In this world

It would be

You and me

Meant to be

Lot to say

To make you stay

Where you go

When you sleep

So in all honesty

If I could

Nature programmes use time-lapse photography to make days, months or years pass by while you watch. In a few seconds, a flower opens or a glacier melts, representing the amount of time we have become accustomed to watching this beautiful thing become a beautiful thing.

I wanted to use that theory to write a song in the process of writing a song. That might not make sense but that was my note to myself and for me it made perfect sense. I didn't have to communicate it further than from one set of my own brain cells to another. I'm just not sure whether this explanation works – but they do say writing about music is like dancing to architecture. If we ever meet, whether you think it does or doesn't, let's have a conversation about it.

I thought of Andy Warhol's screen shots, where he would film a subject with no script or agenda apart from capturing a blink or a squint – a natural reaction to what was happening at that very moment.

I really love to make my own dreamy notions about someone else's song and these can sometimes be ruined by the writer themselves pontificating about their work. I hope I have not just done that for you.

Our A&R person jokingly renamed this, 'Not A Lot to Say'. I took it as a compliment: the lack of lyrics did not take anything away from the song.

# 'OH MEN'

*SAME LANGUAGE, DIFFERENT WORLDS, 2016*

Oh men
Work with what they're given
Even in the darker days
Before men were men

The man you knew
Has become his father now
His eyes were not quite as blue
Nor his hand so steady

In a small room where the furniture's polite
We sit side by side
Keep me guessing
Your sentences I like
Good to be precise

We'll grow on and on and I want to know

In the same room
Widow's candles burning bright
Now stand by his side
He was a strong man
Now it's your time to be right, right all right
All right

Oh men
Work with what they're given
Oh men

We grow on and on and I've got to know
We'll go on and on and I want to go
We go on and on and I want to know

Oh men
Oh men

Some songs start with one writer and can end up with more as they go. One such was 'Oh Men'. It started at home with an acoustic guitar and me singing different lyrics, with the word 'ocean' being a placeholder for what would become 'Oh Men'. The acoustic guitar version then went to Kurt Wagner after the sessions for *Oh No I Love You*. He added:

Oh men
Work with what they're given
Even in the darker days
Before men were men

The man you knew
Has become his father now
His eyes were not quite as blue
Nor his hand so steady

And it started to become quite a different entity, not quite one of my songs and not quite one of Kurt Wagner's songs. I sent the track to New York composer Peter Gordon, who lifted the whole thing with an arrangement that really captured the mood of the song. It exists somewhere in the triangle that connects Norfolk to Nashville to New York. It's one of my favourite songs to perform live and one that I feel proudest to have had a part in writing.

# 'TEMPERATURE HIGH'

*SAME LANGUAGE, DIFFERENT WORLDS, 2016*

Temperature's high
We don't know what we are doing here
All that we need is some time
If you agree
Just call me
Like anytime


Comforting ourselves
We're under the same sky
As always time will tell
Oh my


We're under the same sky
We're under the same sky


Just a pause
It is so bright here whatever you say
We have been waiting for today all our lives
Maybe
Let's see
What's possible
Before


Comforting ourselves
We're under the same sky
As always time will tell
Oh my


We're under the same sky
We're under the same sky
We're under the same sky
We're under the same sky

It was the day after The Charlatans had played in Manhattan and I had an arrangement to meet Peter Gordon with the intention to write a song – a song that as yet had no words and no music.

It was a hot day, the hottest in my memory, and I had a flight booked for the following day, but in a way there was no pressure. Sometimes painters just can't paint and runners just can't run, and you can never let a creative block get you too down.

The ingredients for a song can be quite varied: an experience from the past, a need to get a point across, or a message to get the attention of someone you like. Your surroundings can play a part and Peter and I had a third songwriter, that New York summer's day.

Peter handed me an out-of-tune guitar, but that didn't matter, and he sat at the piano next to a window that overlooked the George Washington bridge. He played along with me and started to throw in discordances. I made some notes. We ate some soup. Friends stopped by – there was an open house – and we slowly worked on the song as the not-so-deadline approached. It still puts a smile on my face to think of it and I would like to think Arthur Russell, a hero of mine and Peter's former bandmate, would like the resulting song.

The opening line was to set the mood and it also became the title of the song. A title can seem obvious as it's often repeated in the chorus, but for me settling on a title is something that mostly happens at the end of the process.

'Under the same sky' was a phrase I had in mind for this album. There were lots of differences in our environments – different time zones with different weather. It was a record about finding the similarities that gave the album the title *Same Language Different, Worlds*.

It was a real thrill to work with many of the people who had worked with Arthur Russell – Peter, Ernie Brookes, Mustafa Khaliq Ahmed, Peter Zummo, Kit Fitzgerald, Bill Ruyle and Larry Salzman came with a history which enticed me.

# 'OCEAN TERMINUS'

*SAME LANGUAGE, DIFFERENT WORLDS, 2016*

Ocean terminus
Ocean terminus

Marry me to the earth
Let me get carried away by the sea
I am with old man Neptune now

Was standing on the sand
Uncover what is lost
The motion is at odds
At the ocean
At the ocean
At the ocean terminus

Ocean terminus
Ocean terminus

Marry me to the earth
Let me get carried away by the sea
I am with old man Neptune now

Was standing on the sand
Uncover what is lost
The motion is at odds
At the ocean
At the ocean
At the ocean terminus

Same language different worlds
Same language different worlds
Same language different worlds

Uncover what is lost
The motion is at odds

At the ocean
The ocean
The ocean terminus

Same language different worlds
Same language different worlds
Same language different worlds
Same language different worlds
Different worlds

Ocean terminus
Ocean terminus . . .

△

As we have gathered, inspiration can come from anywhere. This particular song was inspired by a destination sign on a bus.

We were driving home after a gig in Edinburgh and on the front of a passing coach were the words 'Ocean terminal'. It sounded like a futuristic place featuring in a sci-fi film. It turned out it was a shopping centre, but in my head the words had anyway been rejigged to 'Ocean terminus'. I repeated the words over and over in my head and realised that the shamanic nature of the sound of them really worked, so the song begins with the repetition of the words numerous times.

I wanted to keep the link with the sea and imagined someone who had given their life to the ocean and dedicated themselves to old man Neptune, like Santiago in Hemingway's *The Old Man and the Sea*.

# 'BEGIN'

*SAME LANGUAGE, DIFFERENT WORLDS, 2016*

Begin
Begin talking, softly
Taking it in

Let the breezes
Cool you

Free from the heartache
Search for new horizons

Taking it in
Let me begin

It never needs to be mentioned
It is just recognised
With so little between
The highs and them damn lows
Sentimental at most
Well measured at best
But taking a chance

On someone like me
On someone like me
On someone like me

Autumn breezes
Summer leaves us

Unearth the magic
Go with what you feel

Taking it in
Let me begin

There's a record I bought
That I've already got
It means so much to me
'Cause I played it a lot
It reminds me so much
Of the place where we met


Oooh
Oooh


Let me begin
Taking it in . . .


△


Collaborative songs can lead to anxiety and it's taken thirty years to fine tune how it works with The Charlatans. With Peter Gordon, I had a transatlantic partnership – I was the Bernie Taupin to his Elton John. Lyrics were sent as files and emails replaced faxes but the remote nature and time zone difference made the writing process really new and exciting. I knew we'd be able to write soundscape-style tracks but I really wanted to write a pop song too.

'Begin' was the beginning of working together. It's about two people who respect each other but don't know what the results of their endeavours will be. It was like the start of a romance, hoping it would go well but understanding that it might not. It's the idea of enjoying being in the moment even when you're not sure which direction it will take you. It's like when two people begin talking: you don't know where it will go, but it's conversation that makes up our lives.


There's a record I bought
That I've already got

It means so much to me
'Cause I played it a lot

This is a reference to my last book, which was about friends recommending albums to buy. I would search them out on vinyl. I already had a few of them but it was no less fun to be diving back in on somebody else's orders.

# 'HEY SUNRISE'

*DIFFERENT DAYS, 2017*

Bathe in
The sunlight
Is everything alright
I bet
Oh yeah

We build
The house together
In freezing cold weather
With the fish
In the tank
To say thanks
Thanks

It's beginning to look like it's light
It's beginning to look like it's quite bright
It's beginning to look like it's light
It's beginning to look like it's quite bright
It's beginning to look like it's light
It's beginning to look like it's quite bright
It's beginning to look like it's light
It's beginning to look like it's my sunrise

In your eyes
Way to go
Let me know
Out of breath
When we met
There at noon
For our debut

It's beginning to look like it's light
It's beginning to look like it's quite bright
It's beginning to look like it's light

It's beginning to look like it's quite bright
It's beginning to look like it's light
It's beginning to look like it's quite bright
It's beginning to look like it's light
It's beginning to look like it's my sunrise

In your eyes
Way to go
Let me know

Hey sunrise
In your eyes
Way to go
Let me know
Hey sunrise
In your eyes
Way to go
Let me know

△

I tried to verbalise the biggest things and the smallest things – from the beautiful hugeness of the sunrise to a goldfish in a bowl.

For decades, I hadn't appreciated the sunrise. It was an unwanted guest, like the previous night had called a cab and fled the scene, leaving the morning in charge. But now it was a youngster needing some milk or some attention. The sunrise was a welcome friend, after an hour or two bumping into things and feeling like the only person who was awake.

The opening lines, 'Bathe in/The sunlight,' was somebody switching a light on, a chance to check that everything was in its place and we were all ready for another day.

'We build the house together/In freezing cold weather' is the matter-of-fact stuff that holds everything together.

'It's beginning to look like it's light/It's beginning to look like it's quite bright' is a mantra for when the blue light before dawn becomes the warm glow of morning.

For ages we could never get it quite right live, but we really wanted to. When that song clicks it's a real emotional one for the band.

# 'SOLUTIONS'

*DIFFERENT DAYS, 2017*

Always running out of time
Building a dream out of reality
Seeking impossibilities
With all eyes upon us

Offering solutions
Desperately seeking solutions
Solutions
Desperately seeking solutions

Always looking for somewhere to rest
Midnight matters shift in the light
Voices speaking in my dreams
Morning so quiet I hear a soft breeze

Offering solutions
Desperately seeking solutions
Solutions
Desperately seeking solutions

Each step
And your first breath
Each step
And your last breath

Always running out of time
Building a dream out of reality
Seeking impossibilities
Morning so quiet I hear a soft breeze

Some songs concern ethereal, universal matters and others everyday mundanities. In 'Solutions' I was thinking of making a five-year plan and wondering what it would be.

It could just as easily have been a few pages in a diary but it came in the form of a song, starting with the title. I was looking for solutions and the phrase came to me as I was thinking – 'Desperately seeking solutions'.

Building a dream out of reality was about taking everything we had and making a future. We were looking over the T-shirts we'd made and into the band's archive, which eventually led to exhibitions in Northwich and Liverpool. It was as much about one stage of the band coming to an end and another one starting, like shedding a skin, only with T-shirts and sweatshirts.

Often people say they have always wanted to be in a band because the life is so carefree. While you're not constrained by the rigmarole of everyday existence, there are more spreadsheets and schedules than you might imagine. This song was an attempt to make the notes of a five-year plan somehow seem more glorious. With hindsight, I don't think it would really stand up as a PowerPoint presentation about future strategies.

# 'PLASTIC MACHINERY'

*DIFFERENT DAYS, 2017*

I too feel the plastic machinery
I know it's hard to be accepted
Our life is just like a dream to me
At times it's good to be rejected

So, let's just run
Even if only in our heads
Leave all of this behind
Unless we could stand still

It's not that we have no interest
It's not that we don't think it's worth it
Oh wait I'm such an idiot
My shoulders find this hard to take in

You can tell me tonight
If not this time
Your thoughts don't need
Don't need to be confined

I feel it too
This broken world
There is no second chance
Our flags unfold

Don't be part of the machinery
I know it's hard to be accepted
Our life is just like a dream to me
At times it's good to be rejected

So let's just run
Even if only in our heads
Leave all of this behind
Unless we could stand still

Oh this machine still working in our heads
Oh this machine still working in our heads

△

Sometimes a lyric comes from words bumping into each other in my head: 'I too feel the plastic machinery' was the first thing I sang while strumming on an acoustic guitar at the Big Mushroom, not sure where the thought had come from.

It is just as likely to be any possible set of words, but as these came to me, the little net that I keep in my brain scooped them up for safe-keeping. The TV and radio news at the time was ultra-confusing. The more we found out about Trump and Brexit the more confusing it became: it was like becoming engulfed in quicksand, when struggling only seemed to make matters worse.

(Note: the feeling of being marginalised reminds me of Thatcher – an unfortunate and difficult time for so many. People need to document the times with songs.)

Imagery from Terry Gilliam's *Brazil* crops up in the chorus . . .

Some people pick up on things that are throwaway comments. 'I am such an idiot' ended up becoming a popular button badge.

# 'DIFFERENT DAYS'

*DIFFERENT DAYS, 2017*

Different days
Nature's gaze
In your headlights

Always the way
When waking up in the dark nights

Was so frightened
Now enlightened
Through distortion
Headless horsemen

Through distortion, through distortion

Different planes
Heading out to the same place
Mapping the skies
I can't wait to see your face

We are all coincidences
Accepting idiosyncrasies
Keep confidences, confidences

I just couldn't say
What it takes to make you laugh
And what it'd take to make you stay
It's not about today
You point to the future
And then you walk away

Like scenes in plays, different days
Different ways, different days

We are all coincidences

Accepting idiosyncrasies
Keep confidences, confidences

I just couldn't say
What it takes to make you laugh
And what it'd take to make you stay
It's not about today
You point to the future
And then you walk away

Like scenes in plays, different days
Different ways, different days
Like scenes in plays, different days
Different ways, different days

△

Whenever a new person came to our house, my mum would pull out a press clipping from the *Northwich Guardian* that described an event which happened sometime in the '80s. Two people from Moulton, the village where we lived, reported a sighting of The – or should I say A – Headless Horseman.

The two people in question were my very own mother and father. They became something of a celebrity power couple in certain aisles of the local supermarket and beyond. As a youngster I was jealous that they'd seen the horseman and, on drives home on dark nights, I'd always be on the lookout, trying to catch a glimpse of him.

The 'distortion' that is mentioned in the lyrics is both the fog on the night but also the glitch in your brain that convinces you that what you thought you saw was real.

'We are all coincidences' came from the idea that nothing changed after the Big Bang. Everything is made from the same material that was around then: the difference between a singer in a band or a wardrobe door is just a matter of chance. I have a list of words for songs and they include 'idiosyncrasies'. It's such a grandiose-sounding word for something that really only describes the foibles we all have as people.

The line, 'You point to the future/And then you walk away,' was something else until a few minutes before we recorded it. The original words didn't quite work and Martin suggested 'and then you walk away'.

'Different Days', the song and album title, were an oblique reference to Trump and Brexit. The reference was to politicians abandoning their commitment and altering their rhetoric as their sagas unfolded – about as close as we get to politics as The Charlatans.

On the night of the recording, while the lyrics were still being written, Sharon Horgan – world-famous comedian and all-round good person – was on the train to Crewe to record some vocals. As we were running through the lines I asked if she would sing the phrase 'Like scenes in plays'.

She said, 'Are you asking me to sing that because I am an actress?' I was about to explain when she started laughing and I realised this was the start of a memorable night's recording. Sharon was funny, generous and patient, and I was proud that our record was the first she had sung on.

# 'SPINNING OUT'

*DIFFERENT DAYS, 2017*

Childhood
Times were loving
With you towering over us

Spinning out
Just like our dads
There are doubts
But I am hoping that they won't last

All those smiling faces
Familiar, every one
Tell me where they go

Wind blows your hair
Rain wets your face
Keep coming back, back to this place

Tastebuds change
It's true
Some things get better with age

Dancing on a stage
Baby needs new shoes
Count the ways
I tried to get back there to you

All those smiling faces
Familiar, every one
Tell me where they go

Trying to get back there again
Trying to get back there again
With you
(sha-na-na-na-na-na-na)

Trying to get back there again
Trying to get back there again
With you
(Baby's got new shoes)

Trying to get back there again
Trying to get back there again
With you
(Baby's got new shoes . . .)

△

It had been an ambition for me to write a song with Paul Weller since 1979 but the chances of that actually happening went up drastically in 1990. The Charlatans had started to be heard by one of our heroes, and then the idea became a real possibility.

From the moment I picked up the phone at Monnow Valley Studio in 1994 to hear Paul Weller's voice enthusing about our song 'Can't Get Out of Bed' and our musical output in general, Paul and I have been friends and he has become something of a mentor. Twenty years after that first conversation, around summer time, we wrote a song together.

Six months earlier, Paul had sent me two instrumentals. We met in Italy at the Umbria Rock Festival, where our bands were playing. A lot happens at festivals: they are open season, spending time with fellow musicians when we all have time to kill. Everyone is relaxed and breezy because we're all doing what we love.

We convened outside his portacabin dressing room and got down to discussing where we were at. He asked me how I was getting on with the song and I put him in the picture. The truth was I hadn't had time to work on it and inspiration hadn't struck. We took that opportunity to compare thoughts and ideas. But it wasn't until I took the flight home that the wheels started turning more quickly. I knew what tempo the lyrics had to fit and I chose the slower song out of the two.

Paul and I were both new fathers, me for the first time, and there was a wistful air to our conversations and when the words came, they came quite quickly. I'd always loved the idea of a song being a story told in about four minutes. There's a famous six-word phrase credited with being a self-contained novel: 'For sale: baby shoes, never worn.' From that line, 'Baby's got new shoes' made it into my notes.

With the passage of time from 1979 to 1990 to 1994, both Paul and I had become so much more like our dads – dancing on a stage wasn't necessarily something that we did, but to me it was a romantic view of our job.

I wanted to capture the feeling of looking through a photo album without getting too schmaltzy. I was nervous when I sent it but was happy with how it sounded. Weller sent a text to let me know that he loved the song. That was maybe my biggest thrill as a songwriter.

# 'INSPIRED AGAIN'

*AS I WAS NOW, 2018*

What goes on in your home
When you're withered and you're alone
Inner silence the night's your own
Coupled only by the telephone
And the pressure's on when you come alone
The proposition of you taking hold

I am the child denied
Every seat but the back of the ride

And I come alone when your temper's gone
I don't want to be inspired again

And all the time we spend inspired again
Reminds us that it never ends
The time we spend inspired again
Reminds us that it never ends

I feel the constant shame
In every language you speak my name
I am the child denied
I don't want to be inspired again

Just like the moth that is so badly burned by the flame
I return again
Just like the moth that is so badly burned by the flame
I don't want to be inspired again

And all the time we spend inspired again
Reminds us that it never ends
The time we spend inspired again
Reminds us that it never ends

It never ends

And all the time we spend inspired again
Reminds us that it never ends
The time we spend inspired again
Reminds us that it never ends
It never ends . . .

△

I was unaware at the age of thirteen that I would become a songwriter. If someone had travelled back in time to tell a younger version of me that I would be a performer, then maybe I would have believed them, but the songs themselves were some kind of beautiful natural occurrence that was to be wondered at rather than deconstructed.

I only ever got to hear the final versions of the recordings of my favourite bands and the interplay of lyrics, melody, arrangement and delivery were overwhelming. I never realised that all the time I spent listening to music was a form of apprenticeship. I am not saying I have ever even got close to the creative heights of Dylan or Lennon, but I certainly picked up some tips through listening to them.

I was told that passing hours and days listening to music was a waste of my time and that I should concentrate on algebra and French vocabulary instead. I'd shrug and just say it was something that I needed to do. I think I was just genuinely avoiding what I should have been doing, but listening to music has served me better than any equations.

# 'CLUTCHING INSIGNIFICANCE'

*AS I WAS NOW*, 2018

Dancing with me intimately
Passionate play, war is the way
Mirror me, I'll put you to sleep
Passing out knives, Swallowing lives

I learned that you were on their side
You're all too quick to compromise
And for a while I was enticed
To walk on water posing as Christ

I liked you before
I liked you before
I liked you before
I liked you before
I liked you before
I met you before
I knew you before
I liked you before

Thick as the thieves
Tugging at sleeves
Dead Siamese
Always the tease
No need to please
Anxiety don't have a key but I guarantee

In uniform we're newly born, it doesn't matter where we're from
Another world the sound of sin
It gave new hope when I was done in

I liked you before
I liked you before
I liked you before
I liked you before

I liked you before
I liked you before
I liked you before
I liked you before

Clutching insignificance, dancing with me
Clutching insignificance, dancing with me

I learned that you were on their side
You're all too quick to compromise
And for a while I was enticed
To walk on water posing as Christ

I liked you before
I liked you before
I liked you before
I liked you before
I liked you before
I liked you before
I liked you before
I liked you before . . .

Clutching insignificance, dancing with me
Clutching insignificance, dancing with me

△

Another one whose title came first. I liked the rhythmic sound of the two words and they seemed to suggest an idea that appealed to me – taking hold of something that had lost meaning and continuing with it anyway, the melancholic feelings of the last vestiges of an emotion, a time or a situation.

I like to think of it as negative positivity – it takes all sorts of things to see us through to the next stage and I am certainly guilty of doing it.

Steffan Halperin, the drummer for the sessions of *As I Was Now*, asked me what my most arrogant lyric was, which I thought was the most fantastic thing to think about. His suggestion was to then 'out-arrogant it'. I thought back and decided that it was 'And come the day I'll be the king/The king of all and everything' from 'With No Shoes'. We went for something to top that: 'and for a while I was enticed/To walk on water posing as Christ'.

The lines are written as various sides of a character. Some are the actual me, some are the shy and nervous me and some are an amplified version of my personality.

My technique for writing songs has changed over the last three decades, which is fairly unsurprising. Various forms of technology such as iPhones have made it easier to make accurate notes of ideas, wherever I might be. I also have a slightly different lifestyle. I've never enjoyed going to the gym – it's not really a natural thing for me to do – but I need a surprising amount of stamina, both physical and mental, to tour and after my failed romance with alcohol, I needed to go somewhere that wasn't a bar.

I found running on a treadmill the least objectionable of the disciplines on offer. I really didn't want to be 'spotting' for fellow weightlifters in gold vests. I liked the solitude of running, to find a place where I could listen to music and, having endured it for a while, I started to enjoy it. The sound of my own feet and the machinery was audible alongside the songs in my headphones and, in addition to favourite tracks on my iPod, I would listen to ideas for songs and put lyrics to them.

I would click the incline to maximum and set the speed to five miles an hour. The resulting lyrics fired out at a similar pace and rhythm – I can always spot my running machine songs. Words for 'Another Version of the Truth' from *As I Was Now*, and 'Begin' from *Same Language, Different Worlds* were both written while running.

*As I Was Now* was an album that hibernated for ten years before being released – a gestation period due to me kind of thinking it had already come out. It was recorded in the lost days between Christmas and New Year in 2008 and then got a bit lost itself until Record Store Day 2018. I had listened to it quite a few times in the interim years and instead of thinking it was dated, it sounded better each time.

# 'ANOTHER VERSION OF THE TRUTH'

*AS I WAS NOW*, 2018

Lately, the kids and I just don't understand
You're always holding flowers in your hand
I guess we're only doing what we can

Maybe it's another version of the truth
A history of the lies you told of youth
The bitter taste of sugar for a tooth

I feel you is what I mean to say
When I do all this will fade away
I've been blind with all that I've seen today
Left behind who we touch don't mind

Don't say, you're only happy when you're in the dirt
And you've forgotten how you used to flirt
I am not the type of person you should hurt

Maybe the flowers you posses are now for me
And I know who it is I am supposed to be
And who it is exactly I should see

I feel you is what I mean to say
When I do all this will fade away
I've been blind with all that I've seen today
Left behind who we touch don't mind
Who we touch don't mind
Who we touch don't mind

I feel you is what I mean to say
When I do all this will fade away
I've been so blind with all that I've seen today
Left behind though now I find
With you I can anticipate
What we'll do
Now I don't have to say
We're aligned with a girl you can't recognise
We have time who we touch don't mind

222

There is a particular headspace I inhabit when I run on a treadmill, and I occupy an equal but opposite headspace when leaving the machinery of the gym behind.

Walking back, into the cold air, regular life rushes through my veins and ideas fill the void of contemplative concentration of the loneliness of the not-so-long-distance runner. The first two lines of this song hit me as I wandered into the car park of the Sunset Boulevard gym I used. I liked the significance of flowers: of blooming, blossoming, and offering something. I identify with the notion of offering something. As I continue to write songs and look for new ideas it is important to keep having something to offer – the flowers leave a trail of petals, a reminder of where I've been, which is one way that I view the songs.

The title represents alternate, but relevant, versions of a story – my life might seem one thing to an onlooker but I know a different reality and I was guessing that the same was the case for lots of people.

This song made it on to the extended version of *Who We Touch* by The Charlatans. We'd recorded it after I played the solo cut, but it didn't make it on to the regular album: I didn't think we'd captured the essence of the song, since much of the eye contact in the studio around this time was a mixture of glares and scowls.

There was a newfound optimism in me as a person and us as a band from *Modern Nature* onwards. We had lost Jon and had recognised it was time to look for the good wherever we could find it. Once I gave the original version of this song a listen, it made me realise that maybe the world needed to hear the rest of the album that, ten years after recording, was given the title *As I Was Now*.

# 'JUST ONE KISS
# (ONE LAST KISS)'

*AS I WAS NOW, 2018*

What would I get for just one kiss
I don't know but I thought it should be like this
What would I give for just one touch
I know what I saw in your eyes they sparkled so much

I don't wanna set anybody free
With childish excuses or apologies
Right from the start I gave you my heart
I did, yes I did, I always wanted to be in love

We sat and watched the summer pass by
As the light would flicker and die

Some people don't know when they're alive
We're all caught up and crushed inside
But I would rather say goodbye
All I have is one wish
You promised one last kiss

What did I get for just one kiss
I never felt my life would end up like this
We can't take our clothes off our hands are too cold
In a horizontal hold there is a story to be told

I know a place where we could hide
Where the lights that flicker inspire

Some people don't know when they're alive
We're all caught up and crushed inside
But I would rather say goodbye

All I have is one wish
You promised one last kiss
All I have is one wish
You promised one last kiss

△

I really love that genre of French chanteuse-style songs by the likes of France Gall and Françoise Hardy. There's a bubblegum innocence to them that encapsulates a moment in time: the Paris riots, Johnny Hallyday, Serge Gainsbourg. I discovered it in my teens, when I became a fan of existential French cinema, as much for the moody settings and the clothes as for the anti-heroes and the bigger themes.

I thought a duet would best capture the spirit and I'd spent some time with Pip Brown, better known to the world as Ladyhawke. I wanted the lyrics to sound like a conversation.

The album was released on Record Store Day and I thought the songs deserved a live outing. I arranged tour dates and that left just the small matter of finding a band. As it turned out, I didn't have to look too far. I'd put out a couple of EPs by Average Sex and I already wanted them to come on the tour. They were down to be the support band, but they learned *As I Was Now* really quickly and played the songs with exactly the energy that was around when I'd first recorded the tracks a decade before. The result on tour was that Average Sex would play their set and then become my backing band for an hour. Their singer, Laetitia, originally from Paris, would join me to sing 'Just One Kiss' as a duet, taking it even closer to its chanteuse-style, Gallic pop roots. Funny how things sometimes work out.

# PLAYLIST

Here are just some of the many songs from which I've drawn inspiration when writing. They're an eclectic mix of music that I love and I guess you can say they've made up the playlist to my songwriting career so far.

The Rolling Stones, 'Dead Flowers'

Prefab Sprout, 'Cars and Girls'

Average Sex, 'Ugly Strangers'

The Members, 'Sound of the Suburbs'

Julie Driscoll, Brian Auger and the Trinity, 'Indian Rope Man'

James Taylor Quartet, 'Blow Up'

The Supremes, 'You Keep Me Hangin' On'

Chuck Wood, 'Seven Days Too Long'

Otis Redding, '(Sittin' On) The Dock of the Bay'

The Byrds, 'Everybody's Been Burned'

The Undertones, 'Teenage Kicks'

Althea and Donna, 'Uptown Top Ranking'

Hans Zimmer, 'True Romance'

Steve Hillage, 'It's All Too Much'

Dr John, 'Gris-Gris Gumbo Ya Ya'

Yoko Ono, 'Mind Train'

Bob Dylan, 'John Wesley Harding'

Primal Scream, 'Space Blues #2'

De La Soul, 'Tread Water'

Neil Young, 'Barstool Blues'

William S. Burroughs and Gus Van Sant, 'Millions of Images'

Method Man and Redman, 'How High'

Wu-Tang Clan, 'Impossible'

Ol' Dirty Bastard, 'Got Your Money'

The Beatles, 'Yesterday'

The Clash, 'Spanish Bombs'

Take That, 'Never Forget'

Tim Burgess, 'We All Need Love'

The Beach Boys, 'God Only Knows'

Chrome, 'Anti-Fade'

New Order, 'Sunrise'

The Human League, 'Circus of Death'

Dionne Warwick, 'Do You Know the Way to San Jose'

R Stevie Moore, 'Sort of Way'

The Charlatans, 'Talking in Tones'

Madonna, 'Into the Groove'

# ACKNOWLEDGEMENTS

Nik Void, the Littlest B, Nick Fraser, Ally Dawkins, Matthew Hamilton, Andreas Campomar and the Little, Brown team. Jim Pearson, Stuart Procter and Sarah Pendrigh, Mum & Dad, Warner Chappell, Kobalt, Big Life, BMG, Copyright Control and all the publishers of my lyrics across the globe. And, of course, my brothers on this fantastic journey, The Charlatans.

# SONG CREDITS

"FLOWER"
Words and Music by JON (GB 2) BAKER,
ROBERT JAMES COLLINS, TIMOTHY
ALLAN BURGESS and MARTIN VICTOR
BLUNT
WARNER CHAPPELL MUSIC LTD (PRS)

"ALWAYS IN MIND" (80% WCM)
Words and Music by BAKER, TIMOTHY
ALLAN BURGESS, JONATHAN THOMAS
BROOKES, MARTIN VICTOR BLUNT and
ROBERT JAMES COLLINS
WARNER CHAPPELL MUSIC LTD (PRS)

"INDIAN ROPE"
Words and Music by ROB COLLINS,
TIMOTHY ALLAN BURGESS and MARTIN
VICTOR BLUNT
WARNER CHAPPELL MUSIC LTD (PRS)

"THE ONLY ONE I KNOW"
Words and Music by TIMOTHY BURGESS,
JON (GB 2) BAKER, MARTIN VICTOR
BLUNT, ROBERT JAMES COLLINS and
JON BROOKES
WARNER CHAPPELL MUSIC LTD (PRS)

"POLAR BEAR"
Words and Music by MARTIN VICTOR
BLUNT, TIMOTHY ALLAN BURGESS, JON
(GB 2) BAKER, ROBERT JAMES COLLINS
and JONATHAN THOMAS BROOKES
WARNER CHAPPELL MUSIC LTD (PRS)

"SPROSTON GREEN"
Words and Music by MARTIN VICTOR
BLUNT, TIMOTHY ALLAN BURGESS,
ROBERT JAMES COLLINS and
JON (GB 2) BAKER
WARNER CHAPPELL MUSIC LTD (PRS)

"WHITE SHIRT"
Words and Music by TIMOTHY ALLAN
BURGESS, MARTIN VICTOR BLUNT and
ROBERT JAMES COLLINS
WARNER CHAPPELL MUSIC LTD (PRS)

"THEN"
Words and Music by MARTIN VICTOR
BLUNT, TIMOTHY ALLAN BURGESS,
ROBERT JAMES COLLINS and JONATHAN
THOMAS BROOKES
WARNER CHAPPELL MUSIC LTD (PRS)

"HAPPEN TO DIE"
Words and Music by MARTIN VICTOR
BLUNT, JONATHAN THOMAS BROOKES,
ROBERT JAMES COLLINS, TIMOTHY
ALLAN BURGESS and JON (GB 2) BAKER
WARNER CHAPPELL MUSIC LTD (PRS)

"WEIRDO"
Words and Music by ROBERT JAMES
COLLINS, JON BROOKES, TIMOTHY
BURGESS and MARTIN VICTOR BLUNT
WARNER CHAPPELL MUSIC LTD (PRS)

"TREMELO SONG"
Words and Music by TIMOTHY ALLAN
BURGESS, ROBERT JAMES COLLINS,
JONATHAN THOMAS BROOKES and
MARTIN VICTOR BLUNT
© 1992 WARNER CHAPPELL MUSIC LTD
(PRS)

"CAN'T GET OUT OF BED"
Words and Music by JON BROOKES, ROBERT
JAMES COLLINS, MARTIN VICTOR
BLUNT, TIMOTHY BURGESS and
MARK VINCENT COLLINS
WARNER CHAPPELL MUSIC LTD (PRS)

"JESUS HAIRDO"
Words and Music by MARK VINCENT
COLLINS, JONATHAN THOMAS
BROOKES, ROBERT JAMES COLLINS,
MARTIN VICTOR BLUNT and
TIMOTHY BURGESS
WARNER CHAPPELL MUSIC LTD (PRS)

"CRASHIN' IN"
Words and Music by ROBERT JAMES
COLLINS, MARK VINCENT COLLINS,
MARTIN VICTOR BLUNT, JONATHAN
THOMAS BROOKES and TIMOTHY ALLAN
BURGESS
WARNER CHAPPELL MUSIC LTD (PRS)

"JUST LOOKING"
Words and Music by MARTIN VICTOR
BLUNT, ROBERT JAMES COLLINS,
TIMOTHY ALLAN BURGESS, MARK
VINCENT COLLINS and
JONATHAN THOMAS BROOKES
WARNER CHAPPELL MUSIC LTD (PRS)

"SOUL SAVER"
Words and Music by MARTIN VICTOR
BLUNT, MARK VINCENT COLLINS,
JONATHAN THOMAS BROOKES, ROBERT
JAMES COLLINS and TIMOTHY ALLAN
BURGESS
WARNER CHAPPELL MUSIC LTD (PRS)

"JUST WHEN YOU'RE THINKING THINGS
OVER"
Words and Music by ROBERT JAMES
COLLINS, TIMOTHY BURGESS, MARTIN
VICTOR BLUNT, JON BROOKES and
MARK VINCENT COLLINS
WARNER CHAPPELL MUSIC LTD (PRS)

"BULLET COMES"
Words and Music by MARK VINCENT
COLLINS, TIMOTHY ALLAN BURGESS,
MARTIN VICTOR BLUNT, ROBERT JAMES
COLLINS and JONATHAN THOMAS
BROOKES
WARNER CHAPPELL MUSIC LTD (PRS)

"TELL EVERYONE"
Words and Music by ROBERT JAMES
COLLINS, JONATHAN THOMAS
BROOKES, TIMOTHY ALLAN BURGESS,
MARTIN VICTOR BLUNT and
MARK VINCENT COLLINS
WARNER CHAPPELL MUSIC LTD (PRS)

"LIFE IS SWEET" (50% WCM)
Words and Music by TOM ROWLANDS,
TIMOTHY BURGESS and EDMUND JOHN
SIMONS
WARNER CHAPPELL MUSIC LTD (PRS)
All rights on behalf of WARNER CHAPPELL
MUSIC LTD

"ONE TO ANOTHER"
Words and Music by JON BROOKES,
TIMOTHY BURGESS, MARK VINCENT
COLLINS, MARTIN VICTOR BLUNT and
ROBERT JAMES COLLINS
WARNER CHAPPELL MUSIC LTD (PRS)

"NORTH COUNTRY BOY"
Words and Music by JON BROOKES, ROBERT
JAMES COLLINS, MARTIN VICTOR
BLUNT, TIMOTHY BURGESS and
MARK VINCENT COLLINS
WARNER CHAPPELL MUSIC LTD (PRS)

"TELLIN' STORIES"
Words and Music by MARK VINCENT
COLLINS, ROBERT JAMES COLLINS, JON
BROOKES, MARTIN VICTOR BLUNT and
TIMOTHY BURGESS
WARNER CHAPPELL MUSIC LTD (PRS)

"DON'T NEED A GUN"
Words and Music by MARK VINCENT
COLLINS, JONATHAN THOMAS
BROOKES, ROBERT JAMES COLLINS,
TIMOTHY ALLAN BURGESS and
MARTIN VICTOR BLUNT
WARNER CHAPPELL MUSIC LTD (PRS)

"HOW HIGH"
Words and Music by ROBERT JAMES
COLLINS, MARK VINCENT COLLINS,
MARTIN VICTOR BLUNT, TIMOTHY
BURGESS and JON BROOKES
WARNER CHAPPELL MUSIC LTD (PRS)

"HOW CAN YOU LEAVE US?"
Words and Music by MARTIN VICTOR
BLUNT, MARK VINCENT COLLINS,
ROBERT JAMES COLLINS, TIMOTHY
ALLAN BURGESS and JONATHAN
THOMAS BROOKES
WARNER CHAPPELL MUSIC LTD (PRS)

"TITLE FIGHT"
Words and Music by MARTIN VICTOR
BLUNT, ROBERT JAMES COLLINS,
JONATHAN THOMAS BROOKES, MARK
VINCENT COLLINS and TIMOTHY ALLAN
BURGESS
WARNER CHAPPELL MUSIC LTD (PRS)

"FOREVER"
Words and Music by ANTHONY PAUL
ROGERS, MARK VINCENT COLLINS, JON
BROOKES, MARTIN VICTOR BLUNT and
TIM BURGESS
WARNER CHAPPELL MUSIC LTD (PRS)

"MY BEAUTIFUL FRIEND"
Words and Music by MARK VINCENT
COLLINS, JON BROOKES, MARTIN
VICTOR BLUNT, ANTHONY PAUL
ROGERS and TIM BURGESS
WARNER CHAPPELL MUSIC LTD (PRS)